To [*handwritten inscription*]
You' g[*et...*]
Live Your Dreams!
[*signature*]

Kill Your Giants

By

David Carruthers

Note: No part of this book is intended to offend or discredit anyone. All examples of this book are written specifically and only to show a destructive way of thinking. Some stories have been changed, and no names are ever mentioned.

Why Kill Your Giants?

- ❏ In 2004, 23 million children in the United States were living in homes without a father.[1]
- ❏ A child living in a single-family household is five times more likely to live below the national poverty line.[2]
- ❏ There are more than 15 million cases of sexually transmitted diseases reported annually, and those who are 15-24 years of age are at the highest risk.[3]

---

[1] *Father's Rock!* (n.d.). Retrieved August 10, 2006, from Father Resource Network Web site: http://www.father.com/article.php?sid=134&mode=nested&order=0.

[2] Fagan, Patrick, F., Rector, Robert, E., (2004). *The Effects of Divorce on America.* Retrieved June 5, 2000, from The Heritage Foundation Family Research Web site: http://www.heritage.org/Research/Family/BG1373.cfm.

[3] Weinstock, H., Berman, S., & Cates, Jr., W. (2004). *Sexually Tranmitted Diseases Among American Youth: Incidence and Prevalence Estimates, 2000.* [Electronic version]. *Perspectives on Sexual and Reproductive Health, 36(1): 6-10.* Retrieved September 4, 2006 from Web site: http://www.guttmacher.org/pubs/journals/3600604.html.

- ❏ Pedophiles are overwhelmingly male. Almost all sex crimes against children are committed by males.[4]
- ❏ 1 in 3 girls and 1 in 5 boys will be sexually victimized by their 18th birthday.[5]
- ❏ Annual economic cost of substance abuse to the U.S. economy is estimated at more than $414 billion.[6]
- ❏ Under-age drinking cost the state of Texas more than $5.5 billion a year. This number includes, but is not limited to, such expenses as uninsured medical costs, property damage, loss of life, and fetal alcohol syndrome, as well as the cost of treatment for alcohol-related medical problems.[7]
- ❏ The social costs of gambling such as increased crime, lost work time, bankruptcies and financial hardships faced by the families of gambling

---

[4] *Pedophiles.* (n.d.). Retrieved September 2, 2006, from Colophon, CLogo Pamphlet, Web site: http://www.clogo.org/Pedophiles/Pedophiles-Colophon.html.

[5] Lear., (February, 1992,). *Sexual Abuse: Men sexually abused as Children* [Electronic version]. *Lear's Magazine*, Retrieved August 12, 2006, from Web site: http://www.menstuff.org/issues/byissue/childsexualabuse.html.

[6] *Facts About Substance Abuse: The Human Cost of Substance Abuse,* (n.d.). Retrieved September 4, 2006, from Innovators Combating Substance Abuse, Web site: http://innovatorsawards.org/facts

[7] *MADD Praises NAS Underage Drinking Report.* (2003, September 10). (n.d.). Retrieved September 4, 2006 from Web site: http://www.jointogether.org/nes/yourturn/ammouncements/2003/madd-praises-nas-underage.html.

addicts, cost the economy as much as $54 billion annually.[8]

---

[8] Grinois, L., E. (2004). *Gambling in America: Costs and Benefits* Retrieved September 4, 2006 from Web site: http://www.news.uiuc.edu/news/04/0308 grinols.html.

The unexamined life is not worth living
— Socrates

This book is dedicated to my son, Jonah Rodriguez, for being an awesome young man and my mentor, Bryan Spriggs, for helping me kill my giants.

Acknowledgments

This book is the product of God's exceeding and abundant grace in my life. My Lord and Savior Jesus Christ, I thank You.

There are many people who have helped me immensely in my journey of life, and I cannot take credit for where I am without acknowledging them. To my wife and queen, Wendelyn Carruthers; my mother, Cynthia Carruthers; my grandmother, Mavis; my children, Latoya, Jonah, Antony and Paige; my sisters, Lisa and Dena, my brother Leslie; my uncles and aunts in England; my mentor, Bryan Spriggs; Bishop Gilbert and Yvonne Thompson; Pastors Agabus and Sonja Lartey; Xulon Publishing; Pastor Andy Thompson; Anthony King, Sonya Greene, Brian Embry, Phyllis Needleman, Arnaya & Chessica, Margaret Gregory, Char Maine Hewitt, Karen and Collin Ricketts, Ronald Ricketts, Pauline Blair, Tyrone Mcintosh, Ryan Braithwaite, Chris & Katani Sumner, Jackie Johnson, Jackie Johnson

(Milton), Kareen and Mike Casey, Lorraine Hughes, Cheryl Dunk, Tahlia , Mark Register, Todd Wigfall, Michelle Wigfall, Kimball Scott, Sylvester Mitchell, Deidre Burrell, Latrice Obina, Mike Myers, Verna Myers, Richard Williamson, Pastor Richard Jackson, John Moore, Karl and Andrea Reid, Nathan Landers, Daphne Jacobs, Coach Dennis Wilson, Coach William Thomas and Coach Dover (MP Pride), Erika-Marie S.Geiss, Annette Boyd, and Jubilee Christian Church and Family Life Fellowship. If there is anyone I forgot, please forgive me and charge it to my head and not to my heart; you know how forgetful I can be.

Table of Contents

Foreword

By Bryan B. Spriggs

"Yes! Even though we will walk through the valley of death's shadow, we will not be afraid of any evil. For you, God, are with us (Ps. 23:4). You will take care of us. You will give us the courage to confront the things that we fear the most. We will never have to run from them again. Now, we can begin to face, the giants that seek to destroy the abundance and favor of the Promised Land. Whether our promised land is a newly experienced fellowship with God or a desire to receive the fullness of the blessings His word has promised, we will be confronted with giants that inevitably must be defeated.

As you read this book, you may identify with or be familiar with many of the author's personal struggles, battles, and eventual conquests. Whenever we contend with the flesh and its many manifestations or giants, we must have a calculated and well thought-out strategy for victory. While reading these memoirs, you will come to a realization that the triumphant person is not only the privileged person who has been carefully nurtured and instructed to make the best choices (and you may know such individuals), but also the neglected or abused person. Yes, even this individual, who, in spite of rejection, abandonment, and exile, learns to take hold of every weapon in the arsenal of the Word of God along with prayerful persistence, can carefully hurl and wield those weapons until the enemy of their soul is annihilated.

This book will become for you one of those weapons. As will be later explained, David, as a teenager in biblical times, gathered stones from a stream, took his slingshot, and ran to battle to meet Goliath. And we, like David, must meet our giants on the battle lines of life. When we get there, we too will gather our smooth stone, which is the authority of God's Word, put the stone in our slingshot, and hurl it at the enemy. It is the author's desire for you to receive revelation from God through the words of this book and prayerfully choose the right stone for the giants in your life to be utterly destroyed. Finally, after you've completed the reading, reflect on your own giants that the enemy has created from your past failures and allow the Lord to guide your future battles to the end that you will be victorious over every giant that God empowers you to kill. Those giants were never meant to live in your Promised Land. God will take care of you. Be encouraged!

INTRODUCTION

What Is a Giant?

Well, I am so glad you asked. According to the American Webster's Dictionary, a giant is a legendary man-like being, one of great importance, power, supernatural size, or strength. But I submit that a giant is anything that impedes you from your spiritual, emotional and financial destiny. This idea could cause some to reflect on the biblical story that gives a potent lesson, the story of the land of Canaan. One day God spoke to Moses commanding the Israelites to go possess the land of Canaan because "I the Lord God am giving you the land this day" (Num. 13:1 NIV). God's orders were to take the land and not to be afraid. He appointed selected men as officials and commanders and reminded them of the victories He gave them in the past. This was again to boost their confidence and increase their boldness.

However, when the Israelites got to the land, they grumbled, complaining that the Lord hated them and accused Him of delivering them into the hands of their enemy. The people reported back to one of the leaders named Caleb that the land was indeed flowing with milk and honey, but that the people who occupied the land were stronger and taller than they were. (Milk and honey signified abundance, prosperity, wellness, and good living). Their view was skewed because they concentrated on what they saw and not on what God had promised. As a result of their disbelief and disobedience in God, they died in the desert and did not obtain the promise land. They allowed fear to dominate their thinking. We can see just by this short story how fear can paralyze you to the point where you shy away from your destiny.

Remember our definition; a giant is anything that impedes you from your spiritual, emotional, or financial destiny. So, there are 3 types of destiny. The spiritual destiny, deals with the fact that God created us to have a relationship with Him and there is a specific purpose he has for you. The second is emotional or relational destiny. This deals with having loving, fulfilling relationships with loves ones, friends and also, being a man or woman of quality character. The final one is financial; making sure you are on a budget and your money is working for you, so you don't struggle and live a life of poverty.

Giants can be negative associations, fears, and a disempowering paradigm, a way of thinking that is destroying your goals, potential, dreams, and purposes. They can be spirits, emotions, personalities, low self-esteem, anger, rage, fear of failure, fear of success, lust, haunting memories, bad relationships, sexual and verbal abuse, abandonment, drugs, alcohol, and the list goes on and on.

Some people call them issues, demons, problems, setbacks, but whatever we decide to name them, we all have them whether we believe it or not. We all deal with giants.

Now that we know what giants are and can be, we must follow up with some questions, such as:

How do we deal with these giants?
How did they develop?
How long have they been there?
How can I kill them?

The first step in successfully resolving a problem is recognizing and admitting that there is a problem. For if you do not see, or if you refuse to look at the problem, you will not be able to flourish into the great man or woman you are supposed to be. You don't want to walk around being a flawed diamond. It is by assessing our giants that we see the areas in our lives that need improvement. It is a key factor in becoming stronger, wiser, and just plain better. It is a beautiful thing when you can look back on your life and see the areas you have conquered and realize that those areas were making you weaker and unattractive. It is imperative that we work on ourselves and remove those giants that impede us from achieving the greatness that has been ordained for us. Each of us has a genius inside of us waiting to be unleashed.

Please know that you are special; you have been fearfully and wonderfully made for a purpose that only you can fulfill. The unique thing about being you is that there is only one you, and no one can do the things you do the way you do. When we learn to tap into the gifts and talents that God has given us, we can live abundantly, but we must remove the giants first.

One songwriter said, "Though there be giants in the land, we will not be afraid; He brought us out to take us into the Promised Land." Let us claim our Promised Land, for our destiny awaits us there; let us fulfill our purpose and kill our giants.

CHAPTER 1

Who Put the Giant There?

*A giant never starts out being a giant;
it grows into one.* — David Carruthers

Some of us have heard it said that in order to know where you are going, you have to know where you have come from. Many like to leave their past in the past but fail to realize that they are repeating habits from their past. You should only put the past behind if you have properly dealt with its issues. One reason people keep making the same mistakes, attracting the same people, and not growing in certain areas is that there are past habits that have not been dealt with. Things do not change "just because"; we have to make a conscious decision and effort to make them change. This is why going back is essential. In doing so, you must answer some important questions:

Why do I feel the way I feel about myself?
What do I think about myself?
How long have I had these feelings?
How do I feel about my past?
How do I feel about my future?
Are my past and future connected? If so, how?
How did this all start?

Going back to the beginning will answer questions that have been submerged in our deep subconscious and help bring the answers to light. If we can find out how a giant was born, then we can understand its pattern and solve the problem. If you never go back to the beginning, then there will always be haunting questions.

Some giants grow from negative experiences with parents, family members, teachers, spouses and so forth. Research shows that a child's personality is formed by the age of six. Our personalities reflect who we are, how we think, how we act, and how we react. The people who spend the most time with us help shape us. That is why parents try to expose children at a young age to many positive environments. However, if children are exposed to negative influences and unhealthy situations, these pictures will linger in their minds. It is out of these influences and mental pictures that positive and negative emotions are manifested.

A giant can often be an emotion, but it may not have started out being a giant. The reason it grows into a giant is because we nurture and feed it. While pride, envy, and fear are natural emotions, their sizes depend on our individual experiences and the internal conversations we have with them. If we were to think about the conversations we have about the many different events in our day or our past, what would we notice about the length of time we spend on the negative ones? What do we say? Words have creative power, and some of the giants that are in our lives are there because of the words that were spoken to us.

Okay, I'll get personal, I was born in Nottingham, England, and my maternal grandmother reared me for seven years. I moved to Boston to live with my mother when I was twelve. My mother left me with my grandmother so she could come to America to obtain a better life. Because my grandmother was rearing me, I called her Mom but, I longed for my mother, as did my sister, but we knew we were going to see her soon for she would periodically write letters. My sister and I lived in a house with our five uncles and two aunts whom we viewed as brothers and sisters. With the exception of one aunt they were all older than we were, so we had a lot of second mothers and fathers. My sister is very smart and always did well in school, unlike me. I got poor and average grades. Therefore, my focus was on sports and being a tough guy like my uncles. My grandfather was dying, and my only memory of him was that of a sick man in a wheelchair, so there was no father figure in my home.

In 1981, I came to the United States to live with my mother. It was hard to leave England, but I looked forward to seeing my mother and starting a new American life. I continued to excel in sports in America but got average grades. I didn't know why but I always felt stupid, slow to understand, and lacking mentally. When I was in my early thirties, my grandmother came from England to visit us in Boston. We were reminiscing about our past, and I started to joke about all the spankings I had received from her as a child. I also expressed how difficult it was for me to retain information and how I felt about it. My grandmother responded by saying she spanked all her children, but she beat me because I was slow. I paused and stared at her with such anger and pain. I said, "You beat me because I was slow? Did you think that worked?" I followed-up by saying, "Do you know the amount of pain and the lack of self-esteem I have carried for years in thinking that I was not smart? Do you realize the hurt I have held because I thought I was stupid?" I had to leave the room, and I began to cry uncontrollably. I was so angry with her. Instead of saying, "He seems to have difficulties learning, so let's get him some help," her method was, "I'll beat him until he gets it." Her perception of me was, "He's dense and slow." Imagine how I was treated! We already know how I was thought of by the one who help reared me. I stayed in the room for quite some time and pondered these thoughts over and over again.

I asked God, "Why?" and "What does all this mean?" At that time I was in therapy, my grandmothers words confirmed that therapy was actually good for me because I now knew where my negative self perception came from. It took a few days to make sense of it all, but it all became clear very rapidly. It was an incredibly defining moment for me. It was at that time that the healing process began, because now I knew where the giant came from. When you don't know where your giant comes from, it is difficult to destroy it because there is a mental wall blocking you from seeing its birth. The mental wall can be anything positive or negative—goals, work, relationships, loneliness—whatever the mental wall is, it needs to be placed in the back of your mind so you can focus on removing the giant. Please note this very important comment: healing begins at a very painful point. Killing giants is not going to be an easy task; it is a process in which you should be patient with yourself but not passive.

The reason you don't want to be passive about removing giants is because of what they produce. For example, if laziness and inconsistency are keeping you from obtaining your degree or opening your own business, then passivity is detrimental because your success is contingent upon you eliminating that giant. Whatever the problem is, we are responsible for our giants. We may not have had total control over how they got there, but we still have to kill them.

Giants can come in the form of sickness or disorders. I was diagnosed with Bipolar Disorder in 1987, and it has held me back enormously. Problems and setbacks are going to come; many will be totally out of our control, and they may produce giants. The point is that now that they are here, what are you going to do about them? Self-awareness does not mean anything unless we take actions toward making changes.

From this story, you can probably see how you can have giants that stem from your past. It is important to realize that your past does not determine your future. What matters is what you will do today! Now I am not saying that the history of the giants is irrelevant. What I am saying is that once you have recognized it, don't stay there and sing sad songs about your current situation. Nobody wants to hear sad songs. (Let's keep it light here.)

Do not wallow in self-pity. Cry your tears; eat some chocolate; process it; and move on to the next stage, removing those suckers. If you are currently feeling bad because you see some of your giants, that's good. Let that bad feeling propel you to change. Remember, you are in control of your emotions, and you can change them almost instantaneously. The next time you are experiencing an emotion you don't like, you can pop in your favorite movie or CD to make you laugh or change your mood. No, it doesn't mean that the problem will go away, but it does show the power of inner control. You need to start speaking to your giants and telling them that they are not going to reside in you any longer. List them by name and begin to see yourself the way you would like to see your-self. The process of change begins now. It only takes one day, and one moment to make a decision to change. Make that decision now, there is no better time! Let nothing stop you from killing your giants, starting today.

CHAPTER 2

The Giant of Pride

*The foundation of content must
spring up in the mind, and he who hath so little
knowledge of human nature as to seek happiness
by changing anything but his own disposition,
will waste his life in fruitless efforts and
multiply the grief he proposes
to remove.* — Samuel Johnson

There are two types of pride. The first one is defined by the American Webster's dictionary as self-respect, dignity, value, and pleasure in achievements. This is good because it helps build self-esteem. To have self-respect is to carry your-self in a manner that is decent. How you dress, look, and speak are a part of your self-worth and dignity.

Looking back on our achievements helps us gain confidence to face greater challenges that will come in the future. People put in a lot of hard work to achieve certain accomplishments, whether it is landing a new job, buying a new home, or getting a certificate or degree. Whatever it is, it should be celebrated, because you have worked hard at it, even if you do it all the time. My daughter gets A's and B's on her report card every semester. Therefore I celebrate with her and try to make a big deal out of it.

We can be hard on ourselves; so it is good to look back and say, "Hey, I did a good job" and speak about the details of why and how you did a good job. Go ahead and toot your own horn. It is a poor frog that does not praise his own pond. We need to take the time out and speak about the accomplishments we have made. Take this time to write down all of the awards, accomplishments, and good deeds you have done. In this book, there are a lot of admonishments about removing the ugly things in our lives, so you're going to need this list later.

Legitimate pride creates balance for the times we don't feel good about ourselves. People take pride in their jobs, cars, relationships and things that are valuable to them. It is important to take pride in the various aspects of our lives. Exhibiting pride is attractive and causes others to take interest and even emulate what you do.

In contrast, false pride is arrogant, defensive, conceited, and condescending. People who rely on false pride want to be presented as diamonds but don't want to go through the fire. People who demonstrate this kind of pride do not want to accept constructive criticism; they change the subject or cut the conversation when they feel offended or upset when told they did something wrong, because they don't want to accept what is being said.

Have you ever found yourself in the presence of someone who thinks he knows it all? No matter how gently you correct him, he still gets offended. Someone who never sees her faults but is an expert psychologist at seeing yours. These are examples of pride in very loud ways, but there are others that are more subtle.

Scenario 1

It is your third date, and things are going extremely well. Every conversation lasts at least three hours; you are completely intrigued by one another, and this night is no different. The weather is nice and cool, with a slight breeze, and his cologne is calling your name. You emerged from the hair salon just two hours ago, so your hair is still intact. However, you notice that he has been driving for some time, trying to find this four-star restaurant. You don't want to ask, "Do you know where you are going?" because you want to give him the benefit of the doubt. You definitely don't want to say with an attitude, "You men never ask for directions, and it is clear that you know we are lost." But you're really hungry, so you decide to say (in a calm, sexy way), "Did you make a wrong turn?" He replies, "Um, no, this is a shortcut."

Five minutes later you are seeing more trees in a residential area, and he stops at the nearest gas station to pick up some water because he is thirsty (yeah, right). You're thinking, "Why didn't you pick up some water before, you passed two 7-Elevens and a Store 24? After the gas station, you notice he makes a U-turn, and you quietly smile. Humility would have asked for directions fifteen minutes ago when he passed the first 7-Eleven store. Pride, however, is going to keep on going, acting like it knows what it really doesn't. Sooner or later, pride will fall and bring destruction.

Problems with Pride

Pride is defensive.

Pride underestimates its opponent.

Pride is selfish and unappreciative.

Pride won't acknowledge when it's wrong.

Pride taints the bigger picture.

Pride Is Defensive

Pride is defensive, and people who are defensive act like they know everything, so you can't tell them anything because they already know. The really sad thing is that you know that they don't know, and you are trying to tell them they don't know, but they won't receive it because they think they already know. To be defensive means to protect, shield, or guard. The problem with this in the emotional sense is that when you try to give a friend advice and he is guarded, it can create a challenging situation. What you say could benefit him; however, because he is so defensive, he cannot see it.

If you are not open to constructive criticism, how can you receive anything? You are putting up walls every time you hear an opinion that is contrary to what you believe! How are you going to learn unless you can be taught and rebuked when you head in a direction that is noxious? Could it be that the reason you are so defensive is that you see issues in your life that you refuse to confront? When others tread on skeletons in your closet, you shy away, change the subject, become infuriated, and begin to concentrate on their imperfections, because you are not ready to deal with yours.

A good rule of thumb is that when someone is talking about you then let the focus be on you; listen to what she is saying, listen to her tone, and watch her body language. If what she has to say is true, then simply thank her and work on whatever the problem is.

Pride Underestimates Its Opponent

The story of David and Goliath is as follows: Goliath, a giant in size, came to fight a representative of Israel. Goliath gave King Saul, the king of Israel a proposition. Because there was great enmity between Israel and the Philistines, Goliath arrogantly said that if one of the Israelites could kill him, then the Philistines would be subject to Israel. But if Goliath killed the Israelite, then the Israelites would be subject to the Philistines.

One day David, a young shepherd boy over heard Goliath's challenge and asked King Saul if he could fight this man. Saul's reply was that David was only a boy, and that Goliath had been fighting since his youth. David replied, "I have killed a bear and a lion to save my sheep and as for this uncircumcised

Philistine, I will treat him in the same manner, plus he defies the armies of God." Saul agreed, but he was still very worried. When Goliath saw David, he despised him, and told him, "Today I will give your flesh to the birds of the air and the beasts of the field to eat!"

As Goliath moved toward David to attack, David ran toward him and threw a stone from his sling, which sank into Goliath's forehead, and he fell, face down. David cut off Goliath's head with Goliath's own sword (1 Sam. 17). Goliath and King Saul underestimated David because he was young and small, so neither of them took him seriously. What these men did not take into account was the relationship that God had with David and His power to work through him. They also did not recognize that David feared no man, but feared God.

How many times have boxers or sports teams underestimated their opponents? How many times do we underestimate our workload, schoolwork, and other people's potential?

The will is incredibly strong and able to shock the world, given the right incentives.

Pride Is Selfish and Unappreciative

Another problem with pride is that it only thinks of itself. It does not take other people's feelings into consideration. One night a lady with whom I had arranged to go on a date did not show, neither did she call. To make matters worse, I had spoken with her that same day and she had given me no indication that anything was amiss. Of course I was upset, but as I was complaining, I noticed some things. One, I automatically assumed she had forgot about me or decided to push me off. I also thought she really did not want to be there, because I believe that people do what they want to do. I therefore, wished she had just been honest and said no from the start. I also thought, "What could have gone wrong in that eight-hour span? Why didn't she call?" Notice all the I's in the last few sentences. I did not give her the benefit of the doubt— maybe something had gone wrong, and it was too personal to share. Maybe there was something about this date that made her uncomfortable, and she did not know how to express it. The point is that at the time my pride was only thinking about me. Pride does not put itself in the other person's shoes or even try to appreciate what might have gone wrong with the other party.

I have seen men refuse to submit to the authority of a police officer or security guard who was just doing his job. I believe men especially have pride issues because often times we let our ego get in the way.

Pride is not appreciative. We should never underestimate the power of a thank-you. When you don't say "thank you," it sends a message that you feel you are entitled to this treatment and that you don't have to acknowledge the deed that was just done, whether great or small.

There is a story in the Bible of how Jesus healed ten people with leprosy. These ten men knew and heard of the miracles Jesus had performed. When they saw Jesus, they stood at a distance and called out in a loud voice, "Jesus, Master, have pity on us!" Out of the ten people who received healing, only one came back to Jesus to thank him. Jesus asked, "Were not all ten cleansed?"—a rhetorical question. Then he said, "Where are the other nine?" Being unappreciative will not go well; it will be remembered, and not to your advantage.

Pride Won't Acknowledge When It's Wrong

One of the problems with pride is that it will not acknowledge when it is wrong. It is very difficult to help people see their own flaws when they think they are always right. It becomes increasingly difficult trying to prove a point to them because they are not open. It is like trying to tell an alcoholic that he needs AA or some sort of counseling, and he replies, "I'm fine" as they opens another bottle of Jack Daniels. When you think of this kind of person, it leads you to think that he is going to have to learn the hard way. And this is correct. Proverbs says that when pride comes, then shame follows, and he who cannot accept correction is not wise (Prov 12:1, 11:2).

A friend of mine was upset when it became mandatory state law to wear seatbelts and made comments like, "I should have a choice as to whether I want to wear seatbelts, or save my life or lose it." OK, I love the power of choice, but I value principles over it. I don't like wearing seatbelts either—they can be very uncomfortable—but if they are going to save my life, then buckle up baby. It is really that simple; the bigger picture is more important than how I feel.

I'm sure a lot of us can think of times when it would have saved us time, money, and pain if we had admitted that we were wrong. I have heard people say that they would not apologize even though they knew they were wrong. That is a perfect picture of someone who is being self-righteous and stubborn. Pride inhibits forgiveness, and when we refuse to forgive, we are the ones who stay in bondage, not the person we won't forgive. Pride also stifles self-aware-ness, humility, and other qualities that we need. It is imperative that we relinquish our feelings and see the disadvantages of false pride.

Pride Taints the Picture

Pride will inhibit you from seeing things clearly, because if you are caught up in your own world, you cannot see what is really happening. One evening I was playing a card game called Spades with a few friends. During the course of the game I made a serious request, asking one player not to talk or gesture over the table to her partner, because as those who play Spades know, that is cheating. It seemed that the first time I made my request; she did not hear me, so I stated it again. She totally ignored me and continued to do exactly what I had asked her not to do. Others noticed that there was an air of tension in the room. Afterwards, my sister and her friend stated to me their distaste for my friend's behavior.

The following day, I told my friend that she offended my sister, her friend, and me. Although she apologized, she did so in a halfhearted manner. I explained to her that her behavior was offensive to three people, but she repeatedly defended her posi-tion, and said it was not her intent to offend, and refused to get into a long discussion over it. I said I understood it was not her intent, but the outcome was that people were upset and offended by her actions. If the outcome far outweighs your intent, then your intent is almost irrelevant. Of course she did not set out to hurt anyone—no one usually does in a relationship or in a game—but things do happen, and when they do, it is the responsibility of the offender to put himself in the other person's shoes and not to defend his position.

If someone tells me that I offended him by something I've said, it is not my place to tell him that he perceived me wrong; his perception is his reality. It is my place, however, to find out why the person felt this way. If you don't take the time to find out why someone feels the way he does and you are defending your intent, then the chances of you offending him again are great. You are not seeing the bigger picture, which is his feelings and not your intent. There is an apology that gets people quickly off your back, and then there is one that understands what went wrong and decides to change to ensure that it does not happen again.

Humility Is Beautiful

To be humble is to show patience, to assume a lowly position. Humility is a beautiful thing, and it is linked with wisdom. People who are humble are constantly learning about their gifts and what goes on around them. They are open to correction because they know that others have led the way. One of the most profound sayings I have read is found in Proverbs where Solomon states that humility comes before honor. That is a nice way of saying if you want accolades and glory there is a cost you are going to have to pay. Humility is aware that it will take some time, sweat, and hard work before certain goals are attained.

You know the saying "No pain, no gain." This is used a lot by sports coaches who want to psych up their players and make them realize that in order to be physically and mentally strong, the body is going to have to be put into subjection by physical labor. Humility recognizes that it is profitable to listen to rebuke and constructive criticism. It also realizes that rebuke and constructive criticism come in many forms — trials, financial hardship, failed tests, divorce, whatever life's winds may blow our way. They teach us to be wise and sensitive to others. While I firmly believe that too many couples don't work hard enough to keep their marriages together and that the divorce rate is too high in this country, I am also sensitive to those who have been through a divorce because I have been through a divorce. Before my experience, I would speak out of ignorance and state that there was just no excuse for divorce.

One of the ways to kill pride is to exercise humility. You see, humility is beautiful because it recognizes it can't do everything on its own. It foresees problems that can arise in the future and makes changes. That's what good businesspeople do. They analyze their cash flow, their books, and the way they manage every aspect of the business, and they make changes. These changes will bring the business more money and make it more profitable.

One of the most simple but powerful means to kill pride is by being humble and accepting other people's counsel. Don't underestimate the friends you have in your life. When they approach you with a problem or an issue they notice in you, try to listen and not get defensive. Embrace constructive criticism. I believe real friends are the ones who will let you know when they see ugly things within you. I heard someone say that God loves me too much to allow me to stay the way I am. There are so many ways God speaks to us about pride and humility, through movies, people, and books like, "Kill Your Giants" . Truly there are thousands of examples from many different sources that tell us of the dangers of pride.

In 1997 Chris Bran Cato wrote a wonderful script for a movie entitled Hoodlum. In this movie there were three gangsters who controlled cash flow in their towns. Dutch, a powerful gangster who controlled a part of New York City, would make his presence felt in Harlem because he wanted to expand his territory. Unfortunately, this was not a good idea because Bumpy, who controlled Harlem, retaliated and killed Dutch's men to gain respect. This resulted in killing sprees between the two gangsters. Lucky Luciano, the third gangster, who had respect from both parties, tried to make peace between Dutch and Bumpy, however, Dutch wasn't having it. His response was, "I ain't doing business with no nigger." Bumpy also rejected Lucky's advice initially, but after seeing Dutch's power, he humbled himself and accepted Luciano's counsel. As a result, Bumpy obtained political connections, more power, and protection from Lucky and other business affiliates. Dutch's pride could not see that Lucky's wisdom would prevail. As a result of Bumpy's humility, he was able to run Harlem without any interruption from outside mobsters. Dutch was already at an advantage, but his pride clouded his thinking. He forgot his position; he failed to see that his clout and experience could not match Lucky's, which is why he disregarded his advice.

We can probably look at some of our friends and relatives, and even ourselves, and see our Dutches. Pride will always fall. The prophet Jeremiah puts it this way: "You have been deceived by the fear you inspire in others and by your own pride. You live in a rock fortress and control the mountain heights. But even if you make your nest among the peaks with the eagles, I will bring you crashing down, says the Lord" (Jer. 49:16 NLT).

This does not have to be the case with us if we embrace humility. Humility is the simplest but most powerful way to kill pride; it is the true and proper way in which promotion comes. It would be wise of you to accept another person's counsel, especially a wise person's. It is time that we start learning from others so we can move to the next level in our emotional destiny.

Scenario 2

It's Game 7 of the American League Championship Series. You're already up 5-2, and you have been dominating the whole game. There are less than two innings left, but your pitching power is slowing down. The game begins to turn slowly, and the Red Sox manager asks you if you're OK to continue with this crucial game that will take you to the World Series. You answer, "Yes." Immediately thereafter, your opponent scores a run, and your manager comes and asks you again if you are still OK to play; you still respond with a yes.

Shortly thereafter, your opponent scores two more runs to tie the game 5-5, and now you're forced to leave because your pride thought you could do something more than you usually can. The end result is that at the bottom of the eleventh inning, the Yankees score, beating the Red Sox 6-5. It was a heartbreaking game, and it was a combination of your pride and the manager's lack of wisdom that lost that game.

Humility is crucial, because it knows when to say, "Stop—I cannot perform to the best of my ability."

If you tell people you can handle a storm, please do not call when the winds get too heavy. By the words of your mouth, you set up mental expectations, and when those expectations are not met, people will become disappointed because you should have exercised wisdom to show restraint. It takes more of a person to say what he cannot do than what he can. When you refuse to be humble, your lessons are harder, and you subject yourself to greater shame and embarrassment.

Let's summarize the things I have just said. If you will not acknowledge that you are wrong, then you are conceited and not open to correction. If you underestimate your opponent, then you are lacking intelligence and later will be brought down for a humiliating fall.

If you always think you are right, then you can't be taught and you have to learn lessons the hard way. If you are selfish and unappreciative, then you would not take others into consideration, and being ungrateful will cut you out of blessings for the future. Lastly, pride displays its ignorance at once:

> Fools have no interest in understanding; they only want to air their own opinions (Prov. 18:2 NLT).

Pride will cause you not to see things clearly. If you can't see clearly, then you don't learn because the whole picture is tainted. If you don't learn, then you don't grow. If you don't grow, then you cannot be at your best, and if you are not at your best, then you are cheating your destiny.

As we can see, there are too many negative flaws with pride for us to ignore. Unfortunately, pride will consistently come in to our lives, through work and relationships and other means, but it must be defeated if our real essence is going to shine. We kill pride with humility and self-awareness, which leads to change. In addition, we should receive counsel from people who are wiser than we are, for he who walks with the wise grows wise (Prov. 13:20). Since we know that pride will come again, the next time it rears it ugly face, tell it, "You are the weakest link! Goodbye!"

CHAPTER 3

The Giant of Fear

God has not given us a spirit of fear,
but he hath given unto us a spirit of power, love,
and of sound mind. (1 Tim. 1:7 KJV)

Do not fear the outcome when you don't
know what the outcome is.
–David Carruthers

One of the most disempowering things about fear is that it has you worrying about or afraid of things that are not even there. Have you ever seen one of those Friday the 13th movies where you have just seen Jason waiting for someone in the basement? After the movie, for days—sometimes months—you are afraid to go into the basement because you have visions of Jason waiting for you. (Yeah, OK, I'm the only one.)

We all know that Jason is not in the woods or the basement. According to Webster, fear defined is an agitated feeling caused by the anticipation or the realization of danger, an uneasy feeling that something may happen contrary to one's hopes. Wow! Notice it's described as a feeling; earlier we discovered that most giants are—feelings, emotions we create. These feelings are caused by anticipation. The definition continues by indicating that something may happen contrary to what we desire. We don't know if it is going to happen, but yet we are scared or worried. Worry and fear are best friends. Their primary job is to hold you in some sort of bondage just like the other giants. The quote "don't fear the outcome when you don't know what the outcome is," is an important one, because bondage is one of fear's primary moves. It has you fearing an outcome that may not even exist.

For example, I once had a 1988 Toyota Camry that ran well; it needed some work, but it took me where I needed to go without problems. One day I noticed that the car would not start right away. I had to start it twice for it to run. This, however, would not happen every day but about once a week. I told myself that I would get it checked out later when I got a little bit more money. As it continued to happen, I started to fear and think, "Man, another problem with this car; it's going to cost me all this money that I don't have."

One night, the car ceased to start. Now forced to check out the problem, I took it to a mechanic who told me the engine failed because there was no oil.

The cost to purchase a rebuilt engine was fifteen hundred dollars, for a problem I could have solved with somewhere between twenty and one hundred dollars for an oil change and a repaired oil leak. Because I let fear dominate my thinking, I procrastinated in getting the car fixed; the fear of getting bad news did not allow me to get the car checked out.

No news is not good news; no news is bad news for you, because it keeps you ignorant and afraid. It is crazy, if you think about it, to fear something that is not there. If you're going to be afraid, at least be afraid of something you can see or feel—otherwise it's a waste of energy. I could have been driving that car right now if I had been proactive and not reactive.

This giant will have you believing things that are not true. When you start believing something, then you begin to activate what you believe. There are people walking around thinking that they are superior to others when they are not. But the reason they carry themselves in this manner is that they fear that you may see the many giants in their lives. So they mask them with their jobs, relationships, money, cars, and whatever else they can present to make you think they have it all together. In actuality, it is very sad, because it is just a fear of being exposed, which is birthed out of pride. Fear is a major force in impeding emotional freedom in relationships.

Disadvantages of Fear

Fear Will Put You on the Defensive

Whether it is a game, a fight, or some other tangible means of opposition, you are always going to perform better if you are on the offensive. In the game of chess, if you play the whole game defensively and are worried about your opponent's moves, then you have already lost. If you step into a ring with a boxer with fear at the start of the fight, and if you carry that with you throughout the fight, then you will lose. If you meet every new endeavor with fear, you put yourself at a huge disadvantage in taking on the task.

There are voices that accompany fear that do not work in your favor. Voices that say, "He's too big" or "I can't"; "We will never make it" or "We don't have the money": "Why bother?" or "I'm not qualified or smart enough"—and the list goes on and on. If you noticed, there is at least one common thread in all of those comments: they're all disempowering. Those comments speak to a negative end and do not allow the mind to process a solution, because the words tell the brain that there are no other options. Most of the time, there are alternatives; you're just not saying the proper things and are not asking the right questions.

There are two Bible stories that I will paraphrase for the sake of making a quick and potent point. In the story of David and Goliath, Goliath who was over nine feet tall, paralyzed more than two hundred thousand Israelites with fear. Not one of those men, including the leader of the army, King Saul, met Goliath's challenge; they bowed to the voices of fear in their minds and not to the voice of their God. Saul's fear of Goliath caused him to forget the prior victories God had given him. It took a shepherd boy named David to accept Goliath's challenge and defeat him.

The other story is in Numbers 13, which I mentioned in the introduction, God told the Israelites to possess the land of Canaan, which was flowing with prosperity. They told their leader, Moses, that yes, the land does flow with milk and honey, but there are giants in the land. They said that they couldn't take the land, because its people were bigger and stronger than the Israelites; in fact, the Israelites said, that they (the Israelites) looked like grasshoppers in comparison to the people of the land. This kind of talk spells out defeat. Almighty God had already told them that the land was their possession, but because they reasoned with their own minds, they retreated and did not enter the land of promise.

You are not supposed to be a defensive player in life but one who takes command and charge of your destiny. Take it!

Fear Deactivates Faith

> Now faith is being sure of what we hope for and certain of what we do not see (Heb. 11:1 NIV).

Can you imagine walking and talking to the Lord Jesus Christ Himself, in the flesh? What an amazing opportunity! The disciples of Jesus had this for a few years. One day they were all on a boat and saw what looked like a ghost walking on the water. Peter noticed that it was Jesus and said, "Lord, if that is you, then bid me to come." Jesus replied, "Come!" and the impossible began to take place. Peter stepped out of the boat and began to walk on water, but then he took his eyes off Jesus and onto the waves and he started to sink. Peter cried out, "Lord, save me!" Jesus replied, "Why did you doubt?" and Peter said, "I was afraid." Peter was already walking on the water, but he allowed his fear to deactivate the faith he was already exhibiting. Fear dilutes the substance that empowers you, which is faith.

To have faith is to simply believe in something that has not yet happened. We need faith to accomplish the dreams and goals that we have and that others have for us. It is impossible to always see the end result, and this is why faith is needed. Many of us have to perform certain job duties that sometimes are quite challenging. It is in those times that, with all the other responsibilities you have, you've said you will accomplish all that is before you regardless of the opposition. Maybe it was because of who you are or maybe because it was a matter of keeping a job. Whatever the incentive was, you still exercised faith to believe something that was not there yet.

Fear Produces Worry

A profound but unfortunate example of fear-producing worry comes from the unfaithful husband who has left some clues or said some things and now fears that his wife will find out that he has been cheating. Or the teenager who has been lying about her whereabouts for the last four weeks and now she has to change her story because her alibi has just been exposed. Or, maybe it's just not a good time in the relationship; things are very hard for the two of you financially, and now you have to tell him that you're pregnant. The fact of the matter is that the fear of the unknown will cause you to worry.

Worry is natural, but Jesus said a powerful thing that is worth mentioning in Matthew 6. He said, "Which one of you can add a single hour to your life by worrying?" He compared people to the birds, pointing out that God takes care of the birds. He asked, "Are you not worth much more than they? In other words, why worry about the things you cannot change?

When you are in a state of worry, it can cause you to panic. This can be a dangerous state, because when we begin to worry our minds are not at peace, then we make foolish decisions. People begin to revert to destructive habits because of worry, and their worry does not let them see any other options. As a result, they sell drugs, prostitute themselves, overeat or begin to spend time with people who do not have their best interest at heart. The worrying cycle is precarious because it dilutes peace. Peace is of paramount importance in our lives, because when we have it, we think more clearly, while worrying can lead to anxiety attacks and heart attacks. Continual worrying is not good for your health. We all need peace in our lives, especially when things get uncertain and hectic. I know from being diagnosed with bipolar disorder what it means to have no peace of mind, and so I value scriptures like Philippians 4:7

(KJV): "Make your request known unto God, and the peace of God which surpasses all understanding will guard your hearts and minds in Christ Jesus."

During times of turmoil and uncertainty in my life, I meditated on scriptures such as these for strength and assurance. I know that scripture is true, but I will say this: they will hold no power in your life if you do not believe.

Fear Creates Procrastination

Remember the story about my 1988 Toyota Camry? You can see how my fear created that procrastination. If we think about it, many of us have stories about how we let fear delay us from pursuing something we know we should have pursued. I have heard too many times from adults that if they had to do it over again, they would have attempted a lot more activities. So just from that comment alone, we can see that fear not only delays, but it also terminates dreams, aspirations and new endeavors.

Bishop T.D. Jakes has said that fear is the assassin of dreams and greatness. Many dreams have been terminated because we have listened to fear's conversations. The "coulda, woulda, shoulda," comments come from not seizing the moment and not acting on the right impulse. One of the problems with procrastination is that it says, "I will wait for tomorrow," but tomorrow never comes. King David waited for months to tell his wife, Bathsheba, that he had her first husband killed. The main reason he eventually told her was that God heavily convicted him and their first son died. David knew why their child had died, but Bathsheba did not, and to clear up the confusion he confessed his sin to her.

Procrastination causes one to act of out of character. Most of us know it is always best to tell the truth, but if it allows us to escape trouble, then we will procrastinate in telling the truth. A number of celebrity or otherwise prominent court cases have shown how people have delayed or escaped punishment because they omitted the truth. But many times, the truth eventually caught up to them. Procrastination works against good judgment and it is the enemy to productivity.

Fear of Money

Everybody loves it, wants it, and needs more of it. Some people don't like to talk about money because it brings out so many different emotions. Others avoid the topic, while some get engulfed in it and talk about it from every angle.

What emotions come up for you concerning money, and why?

I grew up in the church, so of course you know I heard the famous phrase, "The love of money is the root of all evil." Don't forget the other one: "It is easier for a camel to go through an eye of a needle than for a rich man to enter the kingdom of heaven." Wow! These are powerful and profound statements that have been used incorrectly by any number of preachers. Those comments have kept me in a poverty state of mind for years. Of course some of that was my fault because I did not study the Scriptures, but trusted the wisdom of those authority figures relaying the message.

The New Testament book of 1 Timothy states that godliness with contentment is great gain and that we should be content with what we have, because we can't take it with us when we die. It further states that people who want to get rich fall into temptation and that it plunges many into ruin and destruction. Only then did Timothy write that the love of money is the root of all evil and causes people to wander from the faith.

Please understand that not everyone who desires to get rich will fall into ruin or some kind of destruction. Some will, for many reasons; one may be a lack of balance in their lives; they've never had money before and are not willing to share it now that they do. Another reason may be a lack of vision; an example of this maybe a person who hits the lottery and within a few years squandered all of his winnings. It is the love of money that is the root of all evil; that means don't make it your God, your all in all. The reason it is the root of all evil is because we get greedy and don't know how to handle it. We let money and getting more of it take priority over our marriages, families, relationships, and whatever else is important.

Money is very creative in power, giving us pleasures that less wealthy people cannot enjoy. It is enticing, attracting beautiful women to ugly men. It can lead to sexual orgies, prenuptial marriage agreements, divorce, and lust.

There is a financial empowerment that is available, but it is necessary to evaluate your associations to money, poverty and riches. How do you see money? How would having a lot of it affect you?

The view that the love of money is the root of all evil, does not mean you shouldn't have it in excess, it simply means that you should make sure that when you come into a place of financial prosperity, you remember to empower and help others, which is the reason for you having a lot of money in the first place.

Let's create a simple list of the advantages and disadvantages of the haves and have nots.

Those Who Have Enough	Those Who Do Not Have Enough
Can live where they want	They live in poor areas
Obtain the best education, attend the best schools	Attend public schools and community colleges
Live in cleaner environments where the crime rates are lower	Live in dirty environments where the crime rates are higher
Enjoy vacations Quality of life is improved	Less money to enjoy vacations Quality of life is poor
Take advantage of investments	Barely have enough money to invest
Possibly living debt free	Thousands of dollars in debt

The lists could go on and on. People who have money usually have more confidence, and their quality of life is improved multiple times. In contrast, the opposite is true for those who do not have money. Financial experts say that working-class people are supposed to have an emergency fund of at least a thousand dollars as well as six to nine months of their salary in the bank in case of lay off or inability to work for some reason. Yet the average American is living from paycheck to paycheck.

Money does not create peace or happiness, but it does enhance our lives and paves a way for peace and happiness to emerge. There is a financial freedom that awaits you, but your beliefs about money must be lucid and healthy for you to take hold of it. Living in poverty is not going to benefit you or anyone around you. Take it from the wisest person who ever lived, Solomon:

> A good man leaves an inheritance for his children's children (Prov. 13:22).

Fear of Intimacy

The Main Event: The Male Ego vs. Vulnerability

Wow! How big is the male ego? I agree, ladies— too big. In our defense, I have created a definition for EGO—Elevating a Gentleman's Opinion. Most of the men I have talked to say that all a man wants at the beginning and the end of the day is to feel like a man.

Men's Health Fitness conducted a study years ago on men and women and found out that the first two needs of a man were sexual fulfillment and financial security. The first two needs for women are emotions and affections. It is a man's nature to desire to dominate, own, and conquer. It is natural for us to be extremely competitive and physical because it is a part of who we are. Men feel good about themselves when they are able to provide, and they feel even better when they are needed.

Unfortunately, over the years many of us have lost the balance of vision between a healthy ego and being egotistic. We have let the cars, money, sex, and the pleasures of life take us away from the most important matters of life; God and family.

Ego has become a masquerade because in the boxing ring of life, society has taught us that ego wins; but in the private moments of our lives, most men would not dare to step into the ring and become vulnerable.

Vulnerability says I have to share my deepest fears with my wife. It says I may have to cry in front of her—and the last thing a man wants to do is cry, especially in front of a woman. If a man cries in public, it usually means that he has exhausted all other possibilities, and you are truly seeing a broken man.

The world has portrayed vulnerability as men's enemy, and we have been fighting a senseless battle for years. The fact of the matter is that vulnerability is our very close friend, one that will propel us to the next emotional level in our lives. The warrior King David was a fearless man in battle, but he knew he could cry to the Lord in times of trouble. In Psalms 139 he said, "Search me, O God, and see if there are any anxious thoughts and offensive or wicked ways in me." David knew that if he let God expose his faults that it would continue to unleash his purpose. In another psalm he said, "I have filled my bed with tears." If you read the book of Psalms you will see that it is loaded with David expressing himself in various ways and in various situations. Men need and want to be held, just as women do; most of us have too much pride to say so, but we do. Furthermore, men want to be able to cry on your shoulder, but if they do, they want to be sure you have the same respect for them and you won't throw any of their weaknesses back in their faces in a time of vulnerable exposure.

The phrases "Men don't cry," "Be a man," "Toughen up," "You whine or express yourself too much" and "You're like a girl" are pure garbage. These statements teach men to hold back their feelings, creating physical tension in their bodies and emotions that they abridge. Then society wonders why our men fill the jail cells because they could not control their anger, when society has subliminally taught men that anger is o.k. to express, but conveying their hurts and disappointments is feminine; while commercials tell our women to spend their days at beauty and spa salons finding new ways to de-stress, live longer, and look younger.

As your referee, I call off the fight with vulnerability, not because you can't win but because you're not supposed to. A lot of men are losing the fight of life because they are not vulnerable. Your ego is a masquerade of strength. Being strong in your ego is creating weakness in your armor. Stop fighting vulnerability; it is your friend and your armor.

The best way to fight fear and any giant is to first see the negative impact that it is having in all the areas in your life. This may be painful to see, especially if you write them down, which I highly recommend. Let that pain drive you instead of thwart you. Pain is a great motivator, simply because nobody likes to feel pain.

One of the basic questions you should ask yourself is, "How can I get rid of this pain?" A lot of us have heard this before, but it bears repeating: the only way to conquer that which you fear is to do what you fear. The Bible says that perfect love casts out all fear and that fear has to do with punishment. In what way, is fear trying to punish you? Recognize that fear comes from the devil and not from God and that you do not have to accept it.

Ways to Conquer Fear

Speak aloud this scripture until you believe it and it becomes a part of you:

God has not given us a spirit of fear, but he has given unto us a spirit of power, a spirit of love and of sound mind (2 Tim. 1:7 KJV).

The only way to conquer fear is to do what you fear.

As you begin to write down what you fear and why, you may realize that some of the things you fear are not worth the energy you were giving them. Also, as you share some fears with your close friends, come up with ways to conquer them.

I have talked about four of the negative things that fear does. Now I will talk about the same thing but in a different light. Allow me to reverse the mode.

Be on the Offensive

If fear puts you on the defensive, then get on the offensive. The offensive strategy is one that says attack. It states that you are in control and that you have a game plan to ensure victory. The offensive player does not have defeat on his or her mind. She is too busy thinking about how she is going to win. The single mother does not look at providing for her child as an option. It is imperative for her child to eat; therefore, she creates ways for her child to be adequately provided for. Offense brings confidence, and confidence heightens your chances for victory. Even if you can't be the part, try and look the part. Confidence is attractive and contagious. When you are aggressive it shows that you are not playing around. You clearly mean business when you are on the offense. You need to let fear know that it is an emotion that will no longer control your life. You are in control because you are in attack mode.

Faith

Regardless of what your spiritual beliefs are, you walk in faith every day. When you make plans to see your significant other, plan trips, sit on a chair, or go to bed, you have no guarantee that you will wake up or that any of your plans will come to pass, and yet you believe that they will come true. In the same way, you need to have faith that you will achieve your dreams. You need to have faith that nothing in your life can or will conquer you. I mean that. Everyone has a story, and there is a reason why you are still alive. One of those reasons is so others can be strengthened and motivated by your story. Your faith can truly move mountains. You have already done it; you just need to think back and give yourself some reminders. Therefore, since you have utilized great faith before, do it again so you can take your place with the eagles and soar.

Don't Worry—Be Happy

You remember that famous song by Bobby McFerrin. It packed a powerful message. It is difficult to tell people not to worry, especially when you are not going through what they are. Everyone interprets pain and trials differently. However, one thing is true no matter how hard the situation is: worrying about it, is not going to do a lick of good. The fact is there are some things you can change and others you cannot. This is where I tell people that when you have a problem that is way more than you can handle, now you are probably giving God the attention He has been wanting from you all along. He really does care, so throw your cares on Him and do not worry.

Do It Now

That is probably the best thing you can say to procrastination. Procrastination creates too many excuses, while doing it now deletes them. "Now" is a powerful word, because it speaks of immediate action. That's what you want in your life, immediate action. Putting these practices in your life will create success in your life now!

It is essential that we remove fear from our lives. It is truly the enemy of greatness. Some are called to be great parents, painters, entrepreneurs, and businesswomen. Whatever your genius is, perform it with passion. Take action steps toward it; quickly recognize the voice of fear, and oppose it. You were meant to soar with the eagles; don't let fear keep you hanging with ducks.

It is a commonly known statistical fact that most people are terrified of public speaking. I can vividly remember my first speech class. I was terrified upon giving my speech, and the proof was that I was sweating like a basketball player who just finished a game. But it did not take long to get used to getting up and speaking in front of people; the more I did it, the easier it became. Sometimes we want these profound mystical ways to conquer certain giants, and a lot of times, the principles we have already heard are sure ways to victory. We just need to hear them again and practice them.

CHAPTER 4

The Giant of Anger

*A fool gives full vent to his anger, but a wise man
keeps himself under control.*
(Prov. 29:11 NIV)

Anger is a natural emotion that we all experience
from time to time. It is perfectly OK to become
angry. As a matter of fact, getting angry is healthy; it
is just another emotional state that must be expressed,
but it must be done correctly. You don't want to be
the kind of person who abridges his emotions and
thwarts how he feels, because all he is doing is
suppressing what will eventually come out. There is
a way to release anger that is authoritative and firm,
and will even create a situation that is favorable for
you without unnecessary intimidation.

Even Jesus got angry. When He saw that the
people were using the Temple as a place for financial

gain, He turned over the moneychangers' tables and shouted, "My house will be a house of prayer, but you have made it into a den of thieves!"

So why is anger so dangerous? Well, as with any other giant, it is what we do with this emotion that makes it dangerous.

How do we handle it?

Do we harbor the feelings that proceed from this emotion?

Do we give it full expression, or do we control it?

Anything that you do not master will sooner or later master you. The question is simply this:

What is mastering us?

This is a very important question to ask, because even if your giant is not listed in this book, that does not mean that there isn't something negative that plagues you on a consistent basis. When you find out what masters you, then you will be able to discern the intricate matters of what goes on inside of you. King David stated in Psalms "Search me, oh God, and know my heart; test me and know my anxious thoughts. See if there is any offensive way in me and lead me in the way everlasting" (Ps. 139:23-24-NIV). The continual process of self- examination will lead you on the path towards mastering your emotions

One of the first Bible stories showing anger between two people was the story of Cain and Abel. In the Bible days it was customary to offer burnt sacrifices to God in thanksgiving to Him. The burnt sacrifice was a clean and unblemished animal, which was killed and offered to God. The smoke from the burnt sacrifice was a symbol of praise from man towards God. Cain and Abel offered their individual sacrifices to God, and Abel's offering was accepted, but Cain's was rejected. As a result of this rejection, Cain became angry with his brother and killed him. God had a conversation with Cain in which he rebuked Cain for his wrongdoing and told him that "sin is crouching at your door," but you must master it (Gen. 4:7-NIV).

This kind of behavior still goes on today in our society. Men and women, young and old have killed, or attempted to kill, and many populate the jail cells because they could not control their anger.

If we take a pragmatic look at anger we can see its many damaging effects and what it can lead to. The scripture quoted at the start of this chapter stated that we should not give full vent to anger. To give something full vent is to give it full expression—no limitations, no inhibitions, just let it have its own way. Webster's dictionary defines anger as the feeling of extreme hostility, wanting to fight back, hatred, and rage. There are no giants, especially anger, which you would want to give full vent to. This scripture is a warning, a potent encouragement to not let anger take preeminence.

Anger can turn into rage. When you are enraged then you are out of control. Almost every time we give full vent to our anger, we regret it. We end up doing and saying things for which we have to apologize.

There are three things that we can never get or take back: words, actions, and time. The words, along with our actions, are lost in time, and the only way to rectify, that which went wrong by our words and actions, is to create new ones. It takes so little effort and time for a person to give into their rage and end up killing, raping, stabbing, yelling, or hurting someone. Because of my previous illness and battles with rejection, I have seen my own anger get way out of control; I was destructive and dangerous. I have witnessed men out of control beating and stomping others; I have seen a teenager hit a grown man with a rod with all his might; I have been the recipient of one too many blows, and thousands are victims of fear and violence that have left permanent scars, all because people could not control their anger.

When you give in to the giant of anger, you are saying that these emotions best suit the situation. Depending on the volume of your actions, you are also stating that there is no other way and this is a hopeless case.

We must realize that anger does not ask enough of the right questions; it just responds. The problem with just responding is, you are now using limited brainpower because you are not thinking. A lot of times there are alternatives that promote a win-win situation, but giving into anger does not create an outcome where both parties are thoroughly satisfied.

When we look at anger, it is prudent that we view some of the ways and reasons anger is created. Earlier I wrote that if we can see how a giant is born, then we can understand its patterns. When you understand your enemy's patterns in a fight, then you can predict his moves, which makes it easier to defeat him because you have studied his strategies. That is what every good coach does before he takes on his next opponent; he examines the way the team will respond in various situations. Then he can come up with a counterattack plan for defending their schemes and defeating their offense.

It is the same with giants. We need an effective plan, a regimen that spells out victory because if the plan is thorough and detailed; it will show us how to conquer. Every good plan has strengths and weaknesses, because your opponent has also studied you. We want to be cognizant of how they act and react so that we may become proactive and develop a plan of attack for defeating giants instead of letting giants defeat us.

How Are Anger and Frustration Produced?
Lack of Understanding and Knowledge
Lack of Vision and Perception
Lack of Finances

Lack of Understanding

Wisdom is the principle thing; therefore get wisdom: and with all thy getting get understanding (Prov. 4:7 KJV).

One of the reasons anger creeps into our discussions or circumstances is a lack of understanding. A continuing process of being misunderstood, misrepresented, and having someone have a flawed understanding of who you are is frustrating. This may be because you are trying to communicate a certain point, and the other person develops a negative opinion of you based on what you are saying. When there is insufficient understanding, there is obviously going to be disagreements. Even if you are alone and there is something you cannot figure out, you will become irritated.

This can run even deeper, because if you do not understand who you are, then you will settle for a destiny that is not God-intended. Maybe your inward anger toward yourself causes you to be lazy, rude, and talk with a vocabulary that is not empowering, because nobody has placed in you a sense of worth.

When people understand who they are, they walk with a confidence that speaks volumes about where they are going in life, and that is transferred into every area of their lives. We're dealing here with three aspects of destiny: spiritual, emotional, and financial. Communication, which is part of the emotions, is just one aspect of your destiny.

So let's say you are in a conversation and realize the other person does not comprehend what you are saying. A wise thing to do at this point is to change your approach so that you may be better received. This may be as simple as changing your tone, rephrasing what you are saying, or taking a break and deciding to continue the conversation later. The seed of anger usually starts small, but grows as a result of repetitive negative actions and emotions. You can see how this can inhibit your emotional destiny.

Lack of Vision

> Where there is no revelation, the people cast
> off restraint (Prov. 29:18-NIV).

A revelation is a vision, and another way anger
is birthed is a lack of vision. Most people don't want
to be a part of something that is not going anywhere.
People like to be associated with something that is
thriving, reaching for higher levels. It is safe to state
that anger is associated with frustration, but the two
words have different meanings. Webster defines
frustration as the inability to attain or see a goal,
to nullify or prevent. When people can't see their
value in a relationship, they get discouraged and then
there is a tendency to leave. And while I agree that
winners do not quit, winners also don't stay in a situation where there is no hope of winning. That is why
great players leave one team and agree to get traded
to another, in anticipation of a championship. People
naturally want to be around leaders and want to be
led into great things. But if people are subjected to
leadership in which they feel there is no compelling
vision, then people will desire a change.

Anger will result when people feel they are
following emotional poverty. There has been a
powerful surge in the number of independent women
in the last decade, but most women do not have a
problem being led by a man who is a good leader. The
scripture above states that people throw off restraint
when there is no vision. In other words, there will be
a lack of order when there is no vision, no sight for

the future, no plan. If we look at the fruits of anger we have violence, hostility, vulgar language, rage, and selfishness, just to name a few, they all have one thing in common: they all lack order. No one in their right mind would tolerate any of these actions because they are inappropriate, unprofessional, and unpleasant. Even if we understood the reasons the emotions were being displayed at the time, we expect more from decent people, which is why when we see these actions we expect an apology shortly thereafter. If we are to minimize and learn to control our anger we must possess the correct vision of others, ourselves, and the situation at hand.

Lack of Finances

If there is anything that will cause frustration in a marriage, a relationship, or in life, it is a lack of cash flow. People will steal, kill, rob, and prostitute their bodies to get more cash. While it is imperative to understand the difference between need and greed, there is an essential need for money. When there is not enough money, frustration results. Probably one of the worst feelings for a man is when he feels like he cannot adequately provide for his family because of a lack of money. This can produce arguments between the husband and wife. Many fights would be solved if there was just more money. I am by no means a financial expert, but there are some basic things that need to be assessed so you can know where you are or should be.

In the area of money, it is crucial to have a plan or budget to determine where you are currently and where you want to be in the future. Remember, without a vision the people perish or cast off restraint. You don't want to be dying financially because you made no plans to secure funds for your future. I have seen too many people try to live a champagne life with a Coca-Cola pocketbook. For example, why are you driving a Cadillac Escalade or a Mercedes-Benz when you have Toyota and Dodge money? Your salary is a little over the poverty line, but you own Coach, Prada, and LV bags. You never save; you buy lunch every day, pay high insurance rates on a car that you don't even own, and that lost thousands of dollars in depreciation the minute you drove it off the lot. Then you wonder why you cannot get ahead.

This is not true of everybody, but my point is you need to budget your money, saving, paying off debt, and getting on a financial plan that will put you ahead. If you reprioritize your finances, maybe, you can pay mortgage instead of rent. Instead of going out to the movies or partying every week, purchase a book on money and finances. Trust me, that book purchase will give you a wealth of information that will save you dollars in the long run. Just in the past five years, through my reading of financial books and self-analysis I realized that I had a poverty mentality and would have ended up poor if I had not changed my ways and thinking. Your financial destiny is in your hands; a lot of money experts out there can help you become financially free and independent. Take advantage of their information; they are set, and you're not.

Does God Get Angry?

Yes. I could leave it at that, but that would not be nice. In the Old Testament books, the children of Israel constantly disobeyed God, which caused Him to become angry. The key word is "disobey," and disobedience is sin. Sin is defined as anything that displeases God. While God is a loving God who will forgive, forget, and show His love, He will not tolerate ongoing sin without repercussions. Please, do not be deceived by the enemy; a man will reap what he sows (Gal.6:7 NIV). God is your Creator, and you were created for a purpose. If you are not in line with the Creator's purpose, then you are out of alignment. We as a society have put God in a box, thinking it is OK to do our own thing. We forget that God first gave us not only the strength to do what we do but also the ability.

In the Old Testament He said, He gave us the power to get wealth, and find out the knowledge of witty inventions (Deut. 8:18; Prov. 8:12). Then in the New Testament, He said He gave gifts to men (Eph 4:7 NIV). In God's omnipotent grace, He will not take the talents away, but that does not mean that you should not serve Him with them. I expect my children to become successful in the area of their intelligence, but I would be extremely disappointed and angry if they were to use their gifts to outwit people, take advantage of them, and exploit the poor.

In the same way, God places talents in us and expects us to utilize our talents for Him and not for our own agenda. We value choice; therefore let us make the right decision and trust the almighty God with our lives. God really does get angry when we disobey His will and His commands, and too many people underestimate that. Please, don't let God be angry with you because your life displays disregard of His ways.

Don't Stay Angry

"If you don't take control of your life, we will." This was the sign near one of Boston's jails. Truer words couldn't be spoken, and this is not only true of anger but of any other giant. Getting angry is one thing, but staying angry is quite another. It is staying there that will produce un-forgiveness. The deceiving thing about not forgiving people is that you think that it is hurting them. In actuality, it is not; it is hurting you.

In the New Testament book of Ephesians, it states "And don't sin by letting anger gain control over you. Don't let the sun go down while you are still angry, for anger gives a mighty foothold to the devil." (Eph. 4:26-27 NLT). This basically means don't let your anger outlast the day. If you are not careful, the days become months and months become years if you allow anger to reside. Do you really think the people you are angry with have not moved on, when they are the ones who have not been hurt? Let it go. It is important that you properly deal with the aftermath of being hurt, but if you do not forgive, you hold your-self in an emotional prison. Let the person go and free your-self. This is a powerful way to kill anger.

Another way to kill anger is self-control. Remember that most giants, including anger, are emotions we create and can control. Self-control is simply the ability to control your-self. That sounds simplistic; however, it does start with knowing that fact. I have done a couple of things that have helped me to gain self-control, and I know they will help you. One is this: I ask, is this person and this situation worth the time and the energy that I am currently giving him or it? By asking these questions, my brain is fed new alternatives to better express my anger or to see if it should be expressed. They are very important questions, because everyone should not get the same kind of response from you. It is usually the people closest to us who get us the most frustrated.

Here is another way that I exert self-control: I will not let anyone take me out of my element. This means I have a boundary. You must create a border for your anger and say, "OK, this is enough." You should not give full vent to your anger; it is just plain unhealthy. You should have a healthy way of expressing yourself in anger that does not take you over the edge. That is called self-control.

I love to watch the presidential debates, because the candidates exhibit great self-control. With the many different issues they debate, it is obvious that they become annoyed with each other and would love to use stronger language than they do, but they don't—not just because they are on TV, but also because they have been trained to channel and control their anger, stick to the point, and answer the questions. It is very commendable to have someone attack you verbally over and over again, and you continue to maintain your composure. There is a way to communicate passion and anger without losing control. I believe that being aware of your emotional state, helps to give you control.

Humility will also crush anger, because when you are humble you are willing to accept a lower position. Anger fights back and says no, it has to be this way. Modesty is highly praised because it is teachable. Humility will give you new ways to channel anger and dispose of it. Meekness will say, "I am sorry" even if you are right.

Sometimes it is not about defending your position as much as it is choosing your battles and keeping the peace. I value peace; therefore I must welcome humility. To be humble at times says that I am broken and in need of help. Anger pushes away help, whereas humility welcomes it. When you are modest, you think of others instead of yourself. Being humble will give you awesome self-control. Proverbs states that better is he who is self-controlled than he who takes a city (Prov. 16:32 NIV).

CHAPTER 5

The Giant of Lust

Death and destruction are never satisfied, neither are the eyes of men. (Prov. 27:20 NIV)

W hen I first read that scripture, I thought it was drastic to compare the dissatisfaction of death and destruction with the eyes of man. However, when I started listening to the mindsets of some of my friends, it all made sense. Edwin Louis Cole said, "Lust desires to get, at the expense of others." It really doesn't care, and it is insatiable. I have watched television shows where men and women say they are addicted to sex. I have seen young women prostitute their bodies to try and satisfy their cravings. I have watched relationships and marriages crumble because one partner could not control his or her desire for sex.

To add insult to injury, our society doesn't help the cause; it only encourages this giant. Movies are filled with sensual love scenes. The more nudity displayed the more extensive and "edgy" they become, the more popularity they receive. Female artists start off nice and innocent. Once they reach the age of 21, their behavior says, "I'm grown up now, so I want to expose my body." They are losing confidence in their natural state. They need the opinion of an executive intent on recreating them. It is not enough knowing that God created them in His image and that they were "fearfully and wonderfully made" (Ps. 139:14).

What happened to loving your body? Or is that not in style this year? People no longer want to wait for marriage to explore the joys of sex. Some people have had so much sex that they're anxious that their future mate may be unable to please them, so they decide to live together beforehand to test it out. Others are not satisfied sexually because they are comparing past performances in past relationships or to what they viewed in the last porn movies they saw.

Many women have allowed money and the pressures of society to dictate to them what is beautiful. We are a society that changes its standards of beauty like the weather. Not so long ago, if you were a dark-skinned man or woman, you were degraded. Black models were rare and seldom recognized, especially in Hollywood. Light-skinned women were "in." A round derriere was considered "too big" and big or full lips were considered "too ethnic." A decade later, round, full lips are considered attractive. Women are now going to tanning salons to get the dark effect and getting all sorts of enhancements. It also used to be that if you were dark, you got only negative attention.

Women would receive compliments like "Oh, you are very attractive for a dark-skinned woman." Later celebrities such as Eddie Murphy, Naomi Campbell, Wesley Snipes and Denzel Washington, all dark-skinned, were all over the big screen and magazines, because society finally woke up to what beauty is. Beauty starts from the inside, and it truly is in the eye of the beholder.

A friend of mine told me of the constant cheating her husband used to do. She mentioned that she would dress in different lingerie every night and make love to him, but he would still cheat on her. She thought she was satisfying him, but she couldn't fulfill his needs because she was contending with a spirit of lust. The spirit of lust is extremely ravenous and addictive; therefore it could never be satisfied.

One man said he did not realize how bound he was by sex until he tried to stop. Pornography sales average $10-$14 billion nation wide.[1] Men have reported on national TV that sometimes they would watch seven to eight hours of pornography, and trying to stop was very difficult. Another man stated that he would go through withdrawal symptoms, such as sweating and headaches.

Lust is never satisfied. It wants a white lover, a black lover, a fat one, a slim one, and the list goes on. When it gets tired, it graduates to having threesomes and then to relations with the same gender. Anything can become natural if you allow it to.

There are two types of lust: The lust of the eye, which deals with things we see that we want (clothes, jewelry, money), and the lust of the flesh, which deals with what our bodies want (food, sex, touch). While there is nothing wrong with these desires, it is the intensity of how badly we need them—and why—that needs to be addressed.

Lust is never OK, because it is attached to a demonic spirit. A spirit is the core to the inner part of the man, the essence and substance of who you are; and any time you have a demonic spirit, negative strongholds are attached to it. This is a giant that must be taken seriously. Too many rape victims develop giants of bitterness, anger, and others that hinder their future relationships because of the lack of self-control from their predators. Lust leads to domination. Men commit most acts of rape; they have a natural tendency to want to dominate. This kind of domination is violent, non-caring, and selfish. It gives men a false sense of power.

A man's need to dominate, usually comes from an area in his life that he does not have control over. In an attempt to regain control, he does so in the area of sex. This is a false sense of power for the initiator. It does not have to be as extreme as rape, but the disadvantages still apply.

Five Disadvantages of Lust

Domination
A False Sense of Power
Selfishness
An Insatiable Desire for More
A Depraved Mind

Domination

It is a commonly known fact that men commit most of the sex crimes. Most men are naturally domineering and desire authority. Their need to dominate comes from an area where there is a lack of either respect or authority, or some aspect of emotion that was not being given. Therefore, the offended will take it by any means necessary. The dominating action is one that says "I am in control; I have the power over you." This attitude magnified in the wrong situation can obviously be very harmful, such as in the example of rape. In a recent two-year period, 787,000 women were the victims of rape, and this figure represents only the rapes that were reported.[2]

A False Sense of Power

It is one thing to have dominion over something or someone who willingness allow it; it is quite another when one is being forced into doing something because of a violent act. People usually want to gain power because power was once taken from them. When power is not controlled, a series of unfortunate events take place by the offender to regain what he thought was taken but in actuality he never had. This is usually done through violence or by whatever means a person chooses.

Selfishness

Edwin Louis Cole describes lust perfectly: lust desires to please self at the expense of others. This can be related to the husband who only thinks about his own sexual needs and not his wife's, or the prostitute who suckers the man for money without performing the task for which she was paid, or the person who steals to satisfy his drug habit, and the list goes on. Lust is not limited to just sex.

An Insatiable Desire for More

Sex is an excellent example of something that is very pleasurable; therefore, you want an unending supply. We live in a society that promotes premarital sex but is shocked at the horrific fact that we have the highest rate ever of sexually transmitted diseases. We are a nation that indulges in too many pleasures. Some of the lifestyles of the rich and famous are based on pure greed and unnecessary excess. Anything that you do not control will eventually control you. God said to Cain (in Gen. 4:7) that "sin is crouching at your door, but you must master it." That sentence can be applied to all giants; they desire to master us, but we must master them.

A Depraved Mind

We all appreciate and have an essential need for pleasure, but where do we draw the line? If lust desires and has an insatiable appetite, then it must be controlled. If it is not controlled, then the mind will accept experiments that are unnatural, and then others will not respect boundaries. We have seen boundaries violated with sex, money, greed, and power. Heinous things happen when lust is not controlled. The Bible refers to this as a depraved mind, meaning crazy or unnatural. It is imperative that we examine ourselves daily to make sure that we are not giving the devil a foothold in our minds. We do this by guarding the gates to our hearts, which are our eyes, ears, and mouths. Proverbs 4:23 NIV states: Above all else, guard your heart, for it is the wellspring of life.

Sex deters you from destiny and clouds good judgment. I was a virgin throughout most of my Christian life, and I got married at a very young age. Because of my immaturity I married the first person I was intimate with. While this is the way it should be, it backfired on me because I was not emotionally ready for marriage. While I did marry for love, the birth of my daughter and sex played a major part in my decision. It caused me to take my focus off God and my career. Many Christians marry at a young age because they are not sexually active, however they are not always emotionally ready for the commitment, thus it causes more problems in the marriage, possibly leading to divorce.

The first two needs of a man are sexual fulfillment and financial security. We like to see and hear that we have performed well. It is our nature as men, but for some, it can be a substitute for the love and nurturing we never had. Since we all desire to be appreciated, sex is a powerful tool in filling that void. The feeling of being sexually satisfied gave me ammunition in the areas of confidence, peace, happiness, and pleasure. Sex provided me comfort and validation, something I did not have in my previous relationships. But if sex is not enjoyed in the correct context, which is marriage, then it will only provide a temporary relief that can distract you from your destiny.

Samson and Delilah

Samson was a man of God who had a mission to destroy the Philistines. No man could match his strength. He was a terror to their army. One day, he met Delilah. He was consumed by her passion. They established a relationship that turned sexual. Now Samson knew from his previous relationships that he should not have any dealings with a Philistine, but passion most certainly cancelled his reason and logic. The secret of Samson's strength was in his hair; it had never been cut.

As the relationship continued, Delilah asked Samson to reveal to her the secret to his strength. He cunningly told her that if anyone tied him up with seven fresh ropes that have not been dried, he would be as weak as any other man. So while he was asleep, she tied him up with seven ropes and yelled out, "Samson, the Philistines are upon you!" He broke the ropes with ease. She was hurt and said, "You have made a fool of me." So she asked him, again only to be deceived again. After being tricked three times by his riddles, she said, "You say you love me, but you will not tell me where your strength lies."

Sex creates intimacy, and this is why women begin to develop expectations. Sex is not just physical for them. As a result of her persistence and his love for her, he told her everything. He said that he had been set apart for God and that his hair had never been cut. If it were cut, he would become weak like any other man. Shortly thereafter, when Samson fell asleep, Delilah cut his hair and shouted, "Samson, the Philistines are upon you!" He thought he would break out like the other times, but the Philistines seized him and gouged out his eyes. God left Samson because of his disobedience to Him, as a result, his strength was gone, and he did not realize it.

Samson's lust had led him to Delilah and away from his destiny. If he stayed in God's will, he would have figured out her intentions. The only reason Delilah had connected with Samson in the first place was that she had been paid by the Philistines to find out the source of his strength.

He submitted to his flesh and not his purpose; his enemy took advantage by taking out his eyes and by making him a slave. It was the Philistines' way of celebrating their triumph over God and Samson. They never had plans to kill him, just to humiliate him. They brought him up from the cellar for their entertainment. Eventually, Samson's hair grew back, and he regained his strength. While he was strapped to the two pillars of the building, he pushed them down. This resulted with Samson killing more than three thousand men, as well as Delilah.

Samson suffered unnecessary turmoil and died an early death because of his disobedience to God. That's what giants usually do; they cause pain, time, money, and heartache that we would never have experienced if we had made better decisions. Samson's death was his greatest victory, but sleeping with Delilah caused his greatest defeat.

Three Ways to Kill Lust

Renew the Mind

> Throw off your old evil nature and your former way of life, which is rotten through and through, full of lust and deception. Instead, there must be a spiritual renewal of your thoughts and attitudes. You must display a new nature because you are a new person, created in God's likeness— righteous, holy and true (Eph. 4:22-24 NLT).

To renew is to do over, revive, remodel, replace, go over, replenish, and restore according to Webster's New World Thesaurus. You must recondition your minds to new thoughts and a new way of thinking. You should try to picture your old way of thinking as dead and destructive, and see yourself placing or gathering new thoughts from the Word of God. This again is going to take some time, but over time you will see that those things that used to attract you, you now will despise. Don't beat yourself up and let condemnation come into your mind if you feel you are not progressing fast enough. Remember, a giant never starts out being a giant; it grows into one. You were practicing certain ways for years, so this new nature will take time to manifest.

Guard Your Gate

> A good person produces good deeds from a good heart, and an evil person produces evil deeds from an evil heart. What ever is in your heart determines what you say (Luke 6:45 NLT).

You must watch the images that you let come into your mind. A big part of renewing your mind is changing your behaviors, which means that you must protect your self by watching what you see and hear. You would not let an intruder into your home or allow your children to see images that would be harmful to their minds. In the same way, you have to watch what enters into your mind. If good things are going to come out of your heart, then you are going to have to plant good things in your heart. What you plant is what you reap.

Deny the Flesh

> So put to death the sinful, earthly things lurking within you. Have nothing to do with sexual immorality, impurity, lust, and evil desires. Don't be greedy, for a greedy person is an idolater, worshiping the things of this world. God's terrible anger will come upon those who do such things (Col. 3:5-6 NLT).

It is pretty obvious that the author of this scripture is making a compelling point, in that our desires need to be put to death. It is imperative that you tell your flesh no. At some point you are going to have to tell the old man, that the new nature, the Spirit of God is now in control and the old nature is dead—even when it's war and you hear the war inside of you. Nevertheless, your new nature can win if you deny the cravings of your flesh and feed your spirit. You accomplish this by watching what you see and hear; the things that you now see and hear should empower your spiritual relationship to walk closer to God.

You don't want to play with lust. While its passion may feel natural and good, it is deadly venom in the end. Lust is like fire and drugs, never satisfied and addictive. Just like we tell children "don't play with fire" and "say no to drugs," you would be wise to treat lust the same way.

CHAPTER 6

Stubborn Silence

I tell you the truth, if anyone says to this mountain,
go throw yourself into the sea, and does not doubt
in his heart but believes what he says will happen;
it will be done for him. Therefore, I tell you
whatever you ask for in prayer, believe that
you have received it and it will be yours.
(Mark 11:23-24 NIV)

Silence These Voices

There are voices that I hear, as loud as thunder
    and pouring rain,
They are familiar to me, because I hear them,
    but to everyone else, I seem strange.
Many of them come to me often and success-
    fully outlast my day,

They are voices of my past and they are here
　　to haunt me,
I wonder can you make them go away.
Because even when I don't want to talk, they
　　come and talk to me,
And when I tell them to go, sometimes they
　　don't want to leave.
Ah forget all that deep stuff, I apologize; let's
　　talk about something else instead,
Let me wow you with my talents and show you
　　what I can do;
Anything to silence these voices in my head.

Now when you see and ask me how I'm doing,
　　I'll smile,
And I will say, hey, things are just fine,
But you really don't wanna know how I'm
　　doing,
And what's really going on inside.
You don't wanna know about these voices I'm
　　hearing,
Because that's just too much work for you to do
Besides, if we were to talk, and you were to be
　　honest,
I'll bet you hear voices too.
I think I've got the solution, a preacher said that
　　Jesus died to set me free,
And if He sets you free, then you are surely free
　　indeed.
Since Jesus gave me authority I can have
　　whatever Jesus said,

> Thank God I think I got the solution to silence
> these voices in my head.
>
> jopála poetry

Rejection is definitely a part of life, with children and especially with adults, but when it comes too early from people of importance, such as parents, teachers, counselors, and family, it has devastating effects on the psyche. Rejection is a silent but influential giant that is very stubborn. It will not leave easily, but once you have overcome rejection, it will be one of the most rewarding feelings you can have. There are voices that accompany rejection, but it is imperative that we listen to what the voices are saying. Sometimes, what we think is the enemy of our soul is God's way of trying to get us to face our giants and conquer them. Continual voices of rejection are detrimental to our future destiny if they are not dealt with.

In contrast there may be something about what the voices are saying that you need to analyze and learn from. Speaking from personal experience, I will candidly say that rejection takes years to overcome because it took years to develop.

Leaving England to join my mother in the United States was hard, because my uncles were my closest friends and my mother and I did not bond too well. My thoughts were, she is a woman; what could she possibly understand about a young boy like me? Our relationship was strained for several years, and growing up became more frustrating because I thought of myself as good kid, but I could not satisfy my mother.

During that time, I found out that my mother had been raped and that I was the product of that rape. As years went on, she and I talked about it briefly but not in serious detail, because it was too painful for her. Years later she explained that while carrying me, her mother rejected her for becoming pregnant at a young age, even though it was not her fault. My mother carried a burden of guilt and shame while carrying me; there was no emotional or financial support. She was the black sheep of the family and was ashamed of herself during the whole pregnancy. She desperately wanted to have an abortion but reconsidered and chose to give me life. However, I was neither planned nor wanted, and every time my mother saw me, it reminded her of the man who had violated her. To add insult to injury, he was her first (From that alone, you can see how giants are birthed).

Studies show that whatever the emotional condition of a mother is during pregnancy, that state is passed on to the child. Therefore, the beginning of rejection started for me at the time of conception. Any time you have a seed, there are fruits that develop and grow from that seed. I know that for a fact, because growing up I suffered from low self-esteem and rejection but never knew how to communicate what I felt and never knew why. Through conversations with my mother and years of self-analysis, I finally realized that some of my giants were the products of some of hers.

The unfortunate events in my mother's life caused her pain and developed her giants that were passed on to me. This chain reaction happens in a lot of families, but it does not have to be the case if you examine and catch behaviors early. Also, it took me more than two decades to realize that there was a serious problem with me emotionally. Obviously, it does not have to take that long to detect something is wrong with your inner man, but with age comes wisdom. In addition, you can carry on with life as normal with suppressed giants and deep issues that are not dealt with. Someone else first creates some of our giants, but we are the ones who are ultimately responsible and have to kill them. My rejection stemmed from the womb and also from not having a father, but what impacted me the most was that he did not stay to build a relationship with his son.

Those thoughts really affected me as I was growing up, because all I wanted was a father to hug me in the rough times and in the moments that I did not understand what was going on with me. I needed guidance; I wanted him there to throw a football or a baseball with me. I missed his presence at my football games and track meets. While my mother was at some of the games, it was not the same. A man needs another man to show him how to be a man and to confirm that he is a man. As much as I needed him, eventually I had to deal with the fact that he may never come around. Accepting this sad fact was difficult but liberating, because it propelled me to move on and forgive him for not being there.

In God's goodness to me, He gave me a part of my freedom in this song:

No Daddy in My Home

I have been blessed with someone, a mother
    who really cares,
Problems we've had, some ups and downs but
    many good times we have shared.
My sisters and I made good company, yet I
    would feel so all alone,
'Cause I was a boy, searching for love and
    there's was no daddy in my home.

There were some nights, I'd sit and cry, the pain
    that I felt was much to bear,
Because I'm going through, I need your
    embrace; what kind of daddy is not there?
Don't get me wrong, mother's the best, but yet I
    would feel so alone,
'Cause I was a young man, searching for love,
    'cause there was no daddy in my home.

These feelings inside I just can't hide
But I've learn to swallow my pride and forgive,
But to this day I just can't understand, neither
    can I seem to see;
Why this man named Daddy, he never came to
    see about me.
So now I'm grown with my family, a beautiful
    wife, yes kids, I have three,

Two girls and a boy and oh what joy my beautiful children bring to me.
One child is my seed, the other two I proudly
love and call my own,
And I am so glad, so very glad 'cause they have
a Daddy in their home.
But something went wrong, so very wrong
'cause now there's no Daddy in their home,
Something went wrong, still I'm alone, still
there's no Daddy in my home.

Writing this song was pretty simple, but trying to
sing the song through was an impossible task without
crying. I had no idea until I sang my own song that
there were still issues that I had with my father and
that I had to let them go. I also noticed through
prayer that my perception of God being my Father
was warped because I had no relationship with my
earthly father. Although I had heard that there was a
connection between how you see God as Father and
your relationship with your earthly father, I never
realized it until after writing this song.

Different events in our lives will cause us to see
things more clearly. Looking back, I can see how
my rejection created emotions that were not healthy.
The fruits of my rejection produced in me anger,
hatred, low self-esteem, and fear. The fear came
about because my father was not the only person
who rejected me. I have had other relationships that
were supposed to work out but did not, and so this
produced a fear of intimacy. In my case, one of the

current fruits was a fear of intimacy, but in others it may work in a totally opposite way.

Because of rejection I began to push certain people away, as if to say, "I'll reject you before you reject me." To reject something, as defined by Webster's dictionary, is to discard as useless. Short, simple but very harsh and powerful. Nobody wants to be told outwardly or in a subtle way that he is useless, but that's what rejection does; it says, "I have no use for you. You are no longer needed or wanted."

Rejection comes in many forms. It derives from broken relationships, terminations from employment, abandonment, being the misfit, and being constantly misunderstood. Rejection is especially hurtful when it comes from the people that are closest to you and those who are suppose to understand you. We can see this picture in the New Testament book of John as he was speaking about Jesus:

> He was in the world, and the world was made through him, and the world did not know him. He came to His own and His own did not receive him (John 1:10-11 NIV).

Most people want to be in an atmosphere where they are known because their actions are predicable and accepted in that environment. When rejection pushes away, people will seek acceptance. The question now arises, "What will you do, and how far will you go, to receive acceptance?" This is a very important question, but what is more relevant is your honest answer. Rejection carries along with it powerful negative voices that are incredibly stubborn; it takes a lot of time for them to leave. Some attempt to silence the voices through sex, others through alcohol, and still others through drugs.

How Do You Silence the Giant of Rejection?

A young man does not join a gang because he enjoys the possibilities of violence, knowing that the same destruction he causes could befall him. His motive is acceptance, because in acceptance there is love and in love there is security. That's why close friends and family are so important. Everyone needs to know that there is a group of people they can always count on, someone or something that is consistent that will give them what they need when they need it.

However, if you're "something or someone" is not healthy, it contributes to a destructive nature. If your something is alcohol or drugs, then it is destroying you. Even the pleasures received from sex will not fill the void, because sex always comes with a price tag. The price tag may be intimacy that you cannot give because of where you are emotionally; it may be commitment or even slavery. A prostitute is enslaved to her pimp, therefore, renders a service on the basis of money and orders from someone else, not on the basis of love.

In John 10:10, Jesus said that the thief (the devil) comes to steal, kill, and destroy. The enemy wants to destroy your life through sinful pleasures that lead to emotional turmoil and heartache. He is a trickster; he shows you the pleasures of sin but never the consequences of sin. Jesus said, "I have come that you might have life, and have it more abundantly" (John 10:10 NIV). That life is not just spiritual life; God wants to enrich your life here on earth. He desires that you be in good health and that your soul prospers. To prosper means to do successfully, and the areas of your soul include your mind, will, imagination, and intellect. God is concerned with your total being.

I would be doing you a terrible disservice if I did not tell you the best way to kill your giants—any of them—is through the power of the Lord Jesus Christ and His word, which is the Bible. That is why I use biblical references. Too many people are trying to conquer their demons through psychology, positive thinking, and other rituals that lack power. While these things are good, they lack the total power you need, which is in Jesus.

What Does Rejection Do?

Rejection produces loneliness, because you feel that no one understands you. This causes some people to withdraw. You close up; most people don't know what you are going through, so what is the use of communicating? If isolated for too long and left to your own thoughts, this produces depression. I know about depression, because having been diagnosed with bipolar disorder, I fell into deep depression, which lead to rumors in high school about my sanity and repeated hospitalizations.

Continual depression leads to suicide. Men are four more times likely to commit suicide than women are. Every ninety minutes in the United

States, a woman commits suicide, but it is estimated that one woman will make a suicide attempt every 78 seconds. Suicide was the third leading cause of death among those who are 15-24 years of age; women attempt suicide twice as much as men, but men most often complete the act.[3] Earlier I quoted John 10:10 that the devil comes to kill, steal, and destroy, and I meant that in the literal sense. I have been suicidal several times, but I never had the guts to carry out what I thought and even verbalized.

It is a demonic mindset for a young man with incredible potential, under twenty years of age, desiring to kill him-self, but that's what rejection does if left alone for too long without empowering opposition. Rejection is the decay to the human potential and a drainer of dreams; it is a mountain of debris that must be removed if you are to be properly cleansed. It also decreases self-worth. It steals away confidence and builds low self-esteem. With these feelings being your mode of operation, it now becomes a laborious process to love you and for you to receive love, because your nature will either question it, or say, "I don't deserve this," so you therefore sabotage love. Rejection pushes away real love not because it wants to but rather because when real love comes, the person is confused. We often revert to old habits, because what is known is comfortable, and the unknown produces fear. These kinds of behaviors lead to the giant of self-sabotage, which comes from unworthiness. With this giant, your actions contradict empowerment or anything that is leading toward prosperity, due to the dominant thinking of a tragic event. Because of these events, your mind constantly tells you that you should feel a certain way and will even reject that which is good in your life, because it does not line up with what you know or feel you deserve. Continual feelings of unworthiness are devastating on the psyche and must be interrupted so healing can begin. I believe there is always light at the end of the tunnel, no matter how dark it may seem. Trials always seem harder than they really are at the time, but we can always look back and see where we gained incredible strength from them—and even laugh at them later.

How Do We Kill Rejection?

Since rejection usually stems from the past, it is important to look into our past. We must see which voices, conversations, and events brought up the emotions that made us feel rejected. When we recognize the disparaging cycles, we can interrupt them and make the necessary changes. Rejection, like any other giant, can only be overcome if you face it and deal with it.

Four Ways to Kill Rejection

Know That You Are Loved

> How great is the love the Father has lavished on us, that we should be called the children of God! And that is what we are (1 John 3:1 NIV)!

God bountifully poured out His love on you so much that He sent His Son to die for you so you might have abundant life. He believed in you before you even believed in yourself. Know that you are a child of the most excellent God, who is King. Remember, that in love there is acceptance, embrace the love that God has for you. You have security in his love. He loves you.

You Have a Great Future and Hope

For I know the plans I have for you, declares the Lord, plans to prosper you and not to harm you, plans to give you a hope and a future (Jer. 29:11 NIV).

When you bow down and submit to the voices of rejection, you are concentrating on your past and not on the wonderful future ahead. Why spend time on a muddy past when you have an amazing future. Your focus and vision is now on things ahead. Your mind should be on influencing your future, not reliving your past.

Your Image Is Beautiful

I praise you because I am fearfully and wonderfully made, your works are wonderful, I know that full well (Ps. 139:14 NIV).

You were made in the image of the almighty God, and everything He made was good. Being made in God's image, states you have the same characteristics that God has, you also posses. This is paramount because it speaks to a great identity and purpose. This should help you crush low self-esteem; your image is first and foremost in God, not in the eyes or opinion of man. It is important to see yourself as beautiful, confident and powerful. You should meditate, rehearse and speak out loud scriptures and phrases that empower you such as," I am fearfully and wonderfully made". Remember, as a man thinks in his heart, so is he (Prov 23:7 NKV).

Fill the House

> When an evil spirit comes out of a man, it goes through arid places seeking rest and does not find it. Then it says, "I will return to the house I left." When it arrives, it finds the house swept clean and put in order. Then it goes and takes seven other spirits more wicked than itself, and they go live there. And the final condition of that man is worse than the first—(Luke 11:24-26 NIV).

This is important, because your mind is like a house and what goes in it, is really up to you. It is very possible that you could have victory in an area of your life and then a year later, that same problem in which you had victory, now has victory over you. The main reason for this is that you did not fill the house. Filling the house means keeping a constant flow of empowering information and actions that will combat the enemy's tactics. You fill the house by reading the bible daily. One chapter of Proverbs a day is excellent because the proverbs teach a lot on wisdom, character and how to deal with people. You should surround yourself with people that will pour into you love, confidence and encouragement. This will be influential in building you up and helping you maximize the person you are, but more importantly the person God intended for you to be.

For an ex-drug addict or alcoholic, there are certain things that they cannot do. One basic thing may be to never enter a bar, especially when they are feeling down and vulnerable. Another may be staying away from former friends that would partake in drugs and alcohol. The people you spend time with, the places you go, and the books you read all play a part in filling the house. You have to create new voices that silence the old ones. It is almost like putting on new garments. You are taking off the old garments of rejection and putting on new clothes. Your new clothes are God's image of you and speaking positive words and meditating on things that will bring you to the next level.

CHAPTER 7

Seven Ways to Kill Your Giants

*What lies behind us and what lies before us
are tiny matters compared to what lies
within us.*—Oliver Wendell Holmes

Number 1: Write Them Down

One way to kill your giants is to write them down. For men, there is nothing mushy or feminine in keeping a journal or writing down your thoughts. Look at it as a business move. In every business you have your strengths and your weaknesses; those who stay in business are the ones who maximize their strengths and minimize their weaknesses. Many businesses don't have written business plans, and the key word is "written." The theory is that if you fail to plan, you have already planned to fail. It is the same with giants. When you write them down, it gives you a visual of what your issues are. It keeps them in front of you and brings reality closer.

Often when the plan is in our heads, it is not clear. The purpose of writing them down is that it makes the issue more difficult to ignore if you see it on paper. Writing something down makes it more valid. You want to make your giant hard to ignore so you will deal with it. Too many people walk around with giants in their lives thinking they are doing fine, when in actuality it is hindering a part of their destiny. You wouldn't drive around in your car if you knew something was seriously wrong with it, so why would you do it to yourself? You are your most valuable asset, not your stocks, house, car, or any other tangible thing.

Get a vision for your giants. A vision is a conceptual view of the purpose. The purpose is to kill your giants, which is easier if they are written down.

We also take things more seriously if they are written in the form of a plan. How many times have you planned to do something but failed to complete it because it wasn't written down? Without a plan, rules, or a format, people tend to do their own thing, which has proven to be detrimental in many ways. The reason a plan is effective is that it reminds you of what you're working toward. Everyone should have short- and long-term goals written down. Once you can begin to check off some of the goals you set, it produces such a sense of accomplishment. It feels good when you can say you are improving in certain areas—and when you do, celebrate and reward yourself.

Don't wait for anyone to pat you on the back for something that you know you did well; it may never happen. Take yourself out to a nice restaurant, buy yourself something nice, or do something special for you. Often we are so hungry for validation that we look to others to provide it, instead of validating ourselves. Many people enter into relationships to receive validation, but if they never learned to appreciate themselves, how can they expect others to appreciate them?

Appreciating yourself and being proud of your achievements creates confidence. People are not drawn to people who lack confidence. Confidence is attractive and it produces a boldness that makes you feel as if you can conquer any challenge that comes your way.

Please take a few minutes right now and write down two different visions.

First, write down the kind of person you want to be.

It does not matter if you are emotionally and mentally there at this moment. This is your vision and what you are working towards. Write down your values, what is important in life. How do you want people to describe you? How do people see you? How do you want them to see you? What do your coworkers think of you—or do you even care? What people say about you is a good indication of the vibes you send out on a daily basis. It doesn't take long for people to form an opinion about you, whether positive or negative. If these things are true, do they represent who you are and how you would like to be perceived, or do you need to alter some things?

Once you have written these things down and answered these questions, take a separate sheet and write a game plan for how you intend to accomplish all this.

Second, write down the vision of where you want to be financially.

If you do not have a plan for your finances, someone else does, and you are probably working for him. Write down the amount of money you want to make and why. The "why" is the driving force behind your motivation. My motivation to make more money is poverty-driven, the fact that I don't like being poor. You cannot live where you want, you cannot go where you want, and you cannot eat and buy what you want. Notice all the negatives. This vision will tie into your career goals and will cause you to meditate on what you do well and how you can create wealth. When we write things down, it becomes a plan. If you don't have a plan, get one quickly. When you write things down, they become clear and organized, and it allows you and others to get more focused on executing the plan that will bring you fulfillment.

Number 2: Accountability

In order for your plans to prosper, you are going to need a little help, and that's where accountability comes in. Tell all your friends, both of them (smile). Get a couple of people you trust, who challenge you and motivate you. The reason you're telling someone is that it makes you accountable. This is empowering because it channels responsibility for them and you. Get a couple of people you're close to, and say, "Hey, these are my issues, and I want you to make sure I'm dealing with them." They'll be glad to help you, and if they're real friends, they've probably told you about your issues already. You want someone to look at the giants with you and give you some pointers.

For some, it may be your mother, father, or spouse. I have a friend who has been my mentor for years and has helped me destroy a lot of my giants. The good thing about a mentoring relationship is that a mentor makes you stay on your "p's" and "q's" You know they are watching you. Mentors consistently challenge you, they are hard on you and they do not allow you to settle for mediocrity. They keep you striving for excellence by affirming the gift that is inside of you because they believe in you. This is the perfect person to tell about your giants. "He who listens to a life-giving rebuke will be at home among the wise" and "plans fail because there is a lack of counsel, but with many advisors they succeed" (Prov. 15:31; 15:22 NIV).

As you begin to put this in place, you will see improvement in your life, because you know you have to answer to someone else. The whole purpose of accountability is to do everything in your power to make your plan work.

Number 3: Stop Complaining

I want to stick a sock in the mouths of some people, because they get on my nerves with all their complaining. We live in a microwave, "I want it now," "I want it my way" society. At the slightest bit of pressure, we either fly away or complain. "It's too hot," "It's too cold," "Man, what's up with all this rain?" Shut up! Why complain about the things you cannot change? Usually, nothing positive comes from complaining.

I admit that life is not fair, even in a public business or theater. Sweet Tanya asks, "Where is the ladies room?" Oh, right behind you to the right. I ask, "Where is the men's room?" Go down three flights of stairs and walk down the hallway, go through the back door, you'll be on Washington Street, at the second set of lights, take a left, at the end of that street, you'll see a door guarded by Pit bulls and Rottweilers, and right behind that door is the men's room. OK, I exaggerated a little bit, but the men's room almost always takes twice as long to get to than the ladies' room.

Even though I'm making light of this, complaining wears people down. Words are powerful, and you don't want to waste them on things you cannot change. Don't Sweat the Small Stuff by Richard Carlson is an excellent book that teaches us how to appreciate life and not worry about menial stuff.

I was dating a woman and asked her what her response would be when it came to arguing about certain subjects. She responded that depending on the seriousness of the subject, she would assess the situa-

tion and say, "David, make love to me." A survey says
that is the number-one answer. Her point was that
she was not going to waste time arguing about petty
things. She responded that we would argue if she felt
I was attacking her character. This is a very good attitude to have, because life is too short to be sweating
the small stuff. Solomon says "it is better to live in the
corner of a roof than share a house with a quarrelsome
wife" (Prov. 21:9 NIV). Complaining stifles creative
energy and empowerment. There's nothing worse
than trying to accomplish a goal and your partner is
complaining about the time you put into it and all the
possible things that could go wrong.

Complaining leads to worry, and worry leads to
fear. Fear has you concerned about things that have
not happened or may not happen. While complaining
is not a giant, it is definitely a symptom of one
and has the potential to hold you back immensely.
Complaining usually, if not always, focuses on the
negative aspects of a situation and displays ungrate-
fulness for whatever you are going through at the
time. Everything happens for a reason and, there are
treasures for you in the midst of the trial. However,
when you complain you decrease your chances of
obtaining the treasure, because complaining alters
your focus.

"Consider it pure joy whenever you face trials
of many kinds, because you know that the testing
of your faith, develops perseverance. Perseverance
must finish its work so that you may be mature, and
complete, not lacking anything" (James 1:2-4 NIV).
It is extremely difficult to count it all joy when you

are suffering. The point is to place your focus on the outcome. In this scripture, the author is encouraging us to change our perspective; not to focus on the hardships, but to focus on what the hardships will produce, which is a boost in faith, building of character, prospect of hope, increase in patience and spiritual and emotional maturity. Leaders focus on the outcome and not only the process, because it is in the process where you learn the lessons.

Number 4: Develop a System

One of my giants is inconsistency. If there is any giant that will hold you back from greatness, it is inconsistency. It is deadly, because you will never reach a goal worth reaching if you are not consistent. Usually, the excuses attached to this are "I don't feel like it" or "I've been very busy and haven't had any time"—the kids, my husband, my wife, and so forth. There are thousands of excuses attached to inconsistency; I know them all too well. At the end of the day, how productive were you? Did you work on anything pertaining to your dreams and talents? Many people feel that after a hard day of work, after eight to ten hours, they should eat, relax, watch television, and get ready for bed to do the same thing all over again the next day. While I agree that this sounds good, this will not lead you to millionaire status or achieving greatness in your dream. If your job is your dream, then this does not apply to you. How many people actually love their jobs? Most of us either do not like our jobs or are not making enough money; we do not have job security or a combination of all of those things. Yet millions do the same thing over again and over again which is insanity. If you're going to be consistent in something, let it be toward your dreams, something that you love to do, otherwise it's drudgery.

I love to see movies in which a person is working on their talent because they know their competition is fierce; movies like 8 Mile where a rapper has a dream of being the best so he works intensely towards reaching his goal. Work on developing a system where you are working on your dream every day. If you cannot do it every day, at least do it a few times a week. Set aside times and days when no one can bother you, where you are free from distraction to work on your gift.

I used to be so disorganized it was disgusting. I could not find important receipts or documents, and almost every day I would misplace my wallet and keys. I began to question myself as to why I could not find anything I needed when I needed it. One day at work, I noticed that everything around me was organized. Reservations were filed and listed in alphabetical order, forms and documents were labeled, and all the pens and markers were in a basket. One day one of my awesome coworkers misplaced an item that was usually kept in one specified area. It was so frustrating, because it caused a lot of chaos and confusion because my "awesome" coworker did not put it back in its place. Then a voice said, "You do this all the time."

The reason for my disorganization was simply that I did not have a system. Sound simple? Let's not overcomplicate or intellectualize things if we do not have to.

If you see a method that has proven to be successful, emulate it. Part of the system I observed from my workplace, I applied at home. I began to file all my papers and documents, which saved me hours of time and created much peace. I used to look at people who were organized in amazement. Now I realize that they just had a system. People would call and ask for my resume, and I would panic. I'd look for it a while, but I could never find it. So I decided to call my friend and asked her if she saved it to a disk. She responded that she had given me the disk, and of course I misplaced it. It took me several months to develop a system, but I knew it was essential to my business, talent and personal growth. It was not just a system of filing papers but one to which I dedicate time to do the things that are important.

If you begin to write down all the results you get from not being consistent, you will have an epiphany. You will see all the negative aspects of being inconsistent and how it stifles you. The way to kill this giant is to reverse the mode. You need to develop a system in which you are constantly working on the things that matters the most.

My music producer says I call him as much as a creditor trying to get his money. If I want to get this music CD and this book complete, I have to stay on some people. No one is going to be as passionate about your vision as you are, and no one should be because you own it, which is why you need to be consistent in working towards your goal. If you are not consistent, you cannot excel. The "mother of skill" is repetition. If you are not maximizing your day, get upset with yourself. Watching television and movies are fine, but how much are you viewing? Is this another excuse to not work your gift? Unless you plan on being another Ebert or Roper, becoming a movie critic is not going to put any money in you pocket. Developing a system is imperative to your success and killing your giants.

Number 5: You Are in Control

Please remember that a giant is nothing but a feeling or an emotion. Do not give it more credit than it deserves. I love to eat quality food, but every now and again I will go on a fast. A fast is when you deny yourself food or some other desired thing in order to get closer to God. It might consist of one meal a day or sometimes just liquids, other times it consists of a full fast. The purpose of a fast is to deny the flesh and let it know that you are in control. The problem with us is that we do not deny ourselves enough pleasures. We confirm that we are sexual beings; so we have sex when and how we want it, but when we contract a sexually transmitted disease we go through physical and emotional turmoil. Too often we give in to what is easy instead of what is important.

There have been days when I was inspired to write at midnight. I would be relaxed on a queen-size bed when my mind would fill with various thoughts, phrases and themes. I had two choices. I could stay in my comfortable bed and lose what material I had, or I could be obedient to the Holy Spirit; get out of bed and write. There have been several times when, I did not record what came to mind at that time, and it was completely lost. Sometimes, it came back but never as powerful as the first time I received it.

A giant only grows into one because of the time and attention we offer it. I can remember saying to a friend that a certain person brings out the worst in me. The fact of the matter is that the worst was already there; they just reminded me of it. No one can make you do anything you do not want to do. When you react negatively, it is your choice and your reaction. You can either teach yourself that these choices are acceptable or you can make a conscious decision to change your reaction. We say that the devil made us do it. He did not make us do anything; he knocked on the door, and we let him in.

We have to start taking responsibility for our own actions. The minute we start blaming others for our actions and reactions, we have made a decision to relinquish our control to them. There will always be issues, people, and problems that will challenge us, but how we respond to them is up to us and determines the outcome of our physical, mental, and spiritual destiny. If I do not like where I am working, what my values are, and how I look, then it's my responsibility to make a change. We are where we are based on the decisions we have made. Every decision you make can propel you to achieve or to retreat to mediocrity.

One day, I was talking to a young man downtown and asked him how he was doing. He responded by saying he was making it, but that the "white man" was holding him down. He continued by stating that the government needs to deal with "reparations" (paying money back to black people for the affects of slavery). I can tell you that he was totally misdirected and talking to the wrong man. I simply told him that as African-Americans, we need to stop looking to the government, or anyone else for that matter, for reparations. We are responsible for our own success or the lack thereof. Furthermore, our forefathers died for our freedom, and a lot of us are abusing that freedom. Many of us, don't take advantage of the numerous educational programs provided, but instead we decide to take the short cut to success through illegal activities rather than committing to dedication and hard work. In addition, I find it repulsive that some abuse their freedom by achieving financial success through music that degrade women, glorify sex, violence and the "bling-bling". Our forefathers fought for respect, dignity and equality but now the same name our slave-masters use to degrade us is now a common slang in which we greet each other. We call our black queens out of their name because we don't know who we are. People who stay in that frame of mind are suffering from an identity crisis. I firmly believe that reparations are for people that are looking for handouts and leaders don't look for handouts. Leaders make things happen, they do not wait for someone to give them anything.

No one is going to come and say, "Hey, David, you have a really nice voice; here's $100,000 to produce an album because I can hear the talent." I have to create a buzz and say, "Hey, I've got something to offer; listen to this song. Do you know of any music producers who will work with local artists?" That is why you have to stay in constant communication with people; it may be the only way to get things accomplished. Always know that you are in control of your destiny. You have to make things happen for you first and foremost. If anything, it should be that your children, wife, husband or parents are the motivating force to your success. Know that you are important and special enough to work on you and your dreams. Be good to yourself; love and invest in yourself, because you're worth it!

Number 6: Nip It Early

Have you ever heard the saying, "Nip it in the bud"? Well, there is no rule that says that you have to let it grow. When you begin to hear yourself saying and doing things that are out of character, stop and correct your behavior before it develops into a bad habit. One of the problems with us is that we allow negative thoughts and actions to creep and linger. We get lazy and settle for less, because what we do is more convenient at the given moment. One of the main reasons people do not keep the weight off is that they do not maintain the same intensity in eating correctly and exercising as they did in the beginning. Therefore, it is imperative to follow your original plan.

I have trained my body so that almost everything I eat is healthy, and when I deviate from that, my digestive system pays the price. This is an awesome reminder of why I developed a system in the first place. The benefit is that your giant never becomes a giant and you never give it a chance to grow. Remember that your mind, body and soul are channels where purity and impurity enters.

It is always better when we resolve issues early because they are much easier to manage. I recall issues in my past relationships that I did not address. They reappeared, only to wreak havoc. If someone offends me, I'm learning to speak about it immediately; instead allowing it to fester and turn into anger. Nipping the offense in the bud, cultivates an atmosphere of control, which leads to triumph over the situation.

Number 7: Do Not Be Afraid to Fail

Failure teaches you not to fear failure, because if you can survive it to fight again, you have not failed. —Harvey Mackey

My mother always told me that nothing beats a failure than a try. Most of us are afraid to fail because of what people might think or say. We can be very hard on ourselves. You would not reprimand a baby because she keeps falling when she tries to walk. It is the same with your business concept, idea, or dream. You have to go out there and try. It's okay to fail. Allow the momentary failure to be a teachable lesson of what you did incorrectly. You have already failed if you have given up on your dreams and visions. A lot of people I talk to either don't have dreams or have allowed the vicissitudes of life to stop them from dreaming. Others, talk about their dreams with incredible passion and conviction and within seconds talk themselves out of their dreams by saying it will never happen because of the lack of money. The reason most businesses are better, bigger, and stronger is that they capitalize on their mistakes. Memorandums, policies, and procedures are written and established when employees and managers alike, make gross errors that have cost the company money. To ensure that it does not occur in the future, new policies are put in place.

We learn from our mistakes. It's OK and a part of life. How many professionals pass their licensing exam the first time around, how many lawyers passed the bar on the first try? We improve by trial and error. There are some things that you must fail at, because that teaches you what you are supposed to be doing. I know my strengths and weaknesses. I have no reason to go to school to become a mathematician or scientist, because I am not talented in those areas. Science does fascinate me, but it's much too complicated. The purpose of failure is to drive you to succeed, not to shy you away from it. What if the thing you want to start is your ticket to prosperity, but you never start because you are afraid to fail? The way to conquer any fear is to do the thing that you fear the most.

CHAPTER 8

Maximize Your Genius

Minimize Your Giants by Maximizing Your Genius

Do you see a man skilled in his work? He will serve before kings; he will not serve before obscure men.
(Prov. 22:29 NIV)

There are seven types of intelligences and talents.[4]

1. Linguistic: the ability to use words fluently and speaks well naturally
2. Mathematical: the ability to understand quantity of numbers or numerical equations naturally
3. Kinesthetic: the ability to moves ones body in rhythm and motion naturally
4. Musical: the ability to sing, write and hear melodic tunes naturally

5. Artistic: the ability to paint, draw or sculpt naturally
6. Interpersonal: the ability to understand others naturally
7. Intrapersonal: the ability to naturally know oneself

Everyone has at least one of these. The question is, which one do you have?

What are you doing with it?

Are you letting it lie dormant?

Are you investing in your gift?

Do you appreciate your talent?

Do you wish you had somebody else's intelligence?

Please take a couple of minutes to contemplate on these questions and answer these questions. Write down your answers. Your answers are important. They will confirm or enlighten who you are, what you do, what you don't do, and why. As I stated in the previous chapter, writing things down brings reality a little closer to us, thus decreases our tendency to ignore the problem, and this is good.

There are four basic and primary ways in which you maximize your genius. The first is to know what your genius, (talent) is. When you don't know what your gift is, then you spend years in the wrong place working for someone or at a company that doesn't know your true value because you don't know your true value. If you're going to maximize your genius, you must know what your genius is. Until you find your true passion, you will spend years in drudgery because you're in the wrong place. I know my true happiness and potential is going to shine when I speak, sing and write. Anything outside of that is just filling time.

The second is vision. Habakkuk 2:2—3 NLT – Then the Lord said to me, "Write my answer in large, clear letters on a tablet, so that a runner can read it and tell everyone else. But these things I plan won't happen right away. Slowly, steadily, surely, the time approaches when the vision will be fulfilled. It seems slow, wait patiently, for it will surely take place. It will not be delayed. "

Notice in this scripture the runner is telling everyone else about the vision. The vision is the dream that God gave you. Your vision is to help and inspire others. Your gift ties into your vision. Universities and colleges were created as a result of someone's vision. The visions were to provide quality education to the public. Thus, the visions were established by setting goals and objectives so that the purpose in which the schools were launch, could be fulfilled; hence, a better quality education. Remember some people just talk about their dreams so, put yourself in the company of those that live them.

The third is action. You must take action for your dream to come true, otherwise it will always remain a dream. The difference between the dreamer and the non dreamer is their actions or the lack thereof. Some talk the talk, while others live out what they talk. Take action.

The final one is mentorship. There should be someone in your life who exemplifies what you want to be. Someone who you can follow and say, I want to do what you do. That person should pour into you. Hey, Jesus had 12 disciples whom he train and said to them "you can do greater things than I do, if you believe. A great leader trains others to emulate what he or she does. Find that mentor and emulate him or her, and in turn, mentor someone else.

Know Thyself

One of the best things you can do for yourself is to know yourself. To know your likes and dislikes is important. You should know what you are good at. Your intelligence is and should be the driving force that unleashes the passion to your destiny. I am convinced, that more than 50 percent of the working population hate their jobs. People go to school and spend thousands of dollars on tuition to end up working forty hours or more at a job they don't enjoy. That does not sound like the American dream to me. If you're going to pay money for something, and spend all this time away from your family and friends, you should be doing what you love. I know it is easier said than done, but most people do not believe in themselves, and they stop dreaming once they become a young adult.

Tony Robbins says that most people don't get what they want because they major in minor things. Everyone has at least one of the seven intelligences so it is your job to find out what that is. It's not hard to do; you probably do it every day subconsciously.

If you're around me for more than an hour you will probably hear a song. Sometimes I'll be walking down the street, and out of nowhere a melody will pop in my head. I will then call myself to record the melody on my answering machine. Why? Well, I value my gift. I'm not sure which song is going to hit it big, but if I never record it then I will never know. I have to value what I have; if I don't value my gifts, then how can I expect other people to value them?

Another reason is that if I keep getting these ideas and don't do anything with them, then that means that I am not ready to utilize my gift. You have to be faithful over the little before you can be ruler over much. For example, there have been times when I have gotten a song or idea and did not record it, and within minutes I lost it. I lost it because I did not place any value on it. You have to treat your gift as special and invest in it. I've taken voice lessons, purchased books, and attended seminars. I want to be good at what I do.

We get numerous ideas per week, if not daily; the question is, what are we doing with them? One man said you know you are before your time when other people are coming out with inventions that you already thought of. Les Brown said being successful is having others pay you for what you do best. Now that's the American way.

If you don't use it, you'll lose it. The awesome thing is that God will never take your talent away, but what is the use of having it if you are not going to use it to empower yourself and others? Your talents are your megabucks; they are your tickets out of the ghetto. Think not? Ask the rappers. Your intelligence is what is going to create your income. I used to think,

"Oh, I wish I was a financial consultant or manager or whatever." I don't cry that any more. I love what I do, because I have this gift for a reason. All the time I was wishing I had someone else's gift I could have been investing into mine. The more you appreciate and work on your talent, the more doors will open up for you and your talents.

The Power of Being Alone

Genius is birthed out of isolation.
—Jonah Rodriguez

I get so disgusted with people on television crying about how they are still single and need to be with someone. Don't get me wrong; marriage and finding your soul mate is beautiful. But so is being single. Can we as a society stop acting as if being alone is a curse? As a result of my divorce, I attended school for massage therapy. It was being fired from my job that enabled me to write this book and focus on my album. Being alone is empowering because it is quiet time with your self.

In this busy, crazy world we can't often hear the genius ideas that God is trying to give us. When you take the time to be alone, you begin to appreciate things you once took for granted. Simple things like lying on the grass on a cool summer night and checking out the stars or attending a movie by yourself with no outside opinion of the movie. Your view of the movie could inspire a song, poem, or book, but it's hard to hear sometimes with the dog barking and your mate running his or her mouth telling you what he or she thought. When we are by ourselves, we get to value ourselves, and our gifts begin to speak to us more and more. Often our gifts are telling us that they have been speaking all along, but we have been too busy to hear them.

Our talents and intelligence are like children; they need attention, and they need to be fed. We feed them with time, money, and practice. I guarantee you that if you spend more time by yourself, your giants will be exposed and your talents will shine through.

The Parable of the Talents

This is a story about a master and his three servants. The master was going on a journey and entrusted his property to his men. A talent in this story is a sum of money. The master gave one of his servant's five talents, the other two talents, and the other one talent, according to his ability. The one who received five talents immediately put his money to work and gained five more. The one who received two did the same and received two more. However, the man who received one talent hid his talent in a safe place to give back to his master, because he knew he was a hard working man.

When the master returned, the man with five talents said, "See, I have taken what you have given me, and I gained five more." His master replied, "Well done, thou good and faithful servant. You have been faithful over few, so I will put you in charge of many." The one with two talents said, "Master, you gave me two talents, and I have doubled it." He replied, "Well done, thou good and faithful servant. You have been faithful over few, so I will put you in charge of many." The man who received one talent said, "Master, I knew that you were a hard working man, so I hid your talent in a safe place to give it back to you, so here it is." The master replied, "You wicked and lazy servant. You knew I was a hard working man, and so you should have invested my money so that when I came back I would receive it with greater return. Take the one talent from him and give it to the one who has five. Then throw that worthless servant out where there is weeping and gnashing of teeth"(Matt. 25:14-30 NIV).

Wow. When I first read this story many years ago, I thought the master was being way too hard on the man with one talent. I also thought it was nice of him to return the one talent back to him. (Thank God I don't think like that any more.) But the moral of this story was that the one-talent man had a chance to invest and double the profit, which was the point of the master giving it to him in the first place. I mean the master could have buried it. The one-talent man didn't even try to invest. He did not use his talent, so he lost it. He was lazy and laziness brings poverty. The master knew this and called him worthless because he did not produce anything; he did not value his gift. Therefore, he took the one talent and gave it to someone he knew would be fruitful with it, which was the man with five talents.

A good question is why give it to the man with five talents and not the man with two talents. Glad you asked! It is because to whom much is given, much is required. Sometimes I am amazed how some people tour the country, write books, appear on talk shows, and in their spare time co-star in a movie. They are faithful with what they have, so they are given more. It is a foundational biblical principle. It is why lenders start you off with a small credit limit. If you can't handle a thousand dollars, what makes you think you can handle ten thousand? If you pay on your lower bill consistently and on time, then they will give you the increase.

Don't let your talent be wasted by not practicing or doing anything with it. Practice what you are good at, attend seminars, purchase books, and continue to find out how you can get even better at your gift. The Bible says he who is skilled in his craft shall serve before kings (Prov 22:29 NIV). The word kings in this scripture mean great men. Don't chase the money; chase your gift, and the money will follow. People will pay you for what you do, and the more you do it, the more ideas will come for you to make money. You need to stop wishing you had someone else's gift work your own. Yours is special; that's why God gave it to you, for you to work it. Your talent is one of the primary ways to kill your giants. By maximizing your gifts you are suffocating your giants.

Positive Words Enter

Words and thoughts are the creative force behind
everything that was and is created.
—David Carruthers

Positive words are the creative force toward greatness. They are the driving force behind destiny. What makes a great coach is that he can motivate his team. An excellent coach motivates his players beyond bad performances and concentrates on the present. So his players have been performing below average for the past twenty minutes; his focus is on now. What is happening now will determine the outcome of the game. The same applies to your life. Your past does not determine your future, so forget about your yesterday. You can't keep crying about what you should have done; what you have is now. What are you doing and saying now?

"Sticks and stones may break my bones, but words will never hurt me"—that's garbage. Words can kill you, spiritually, emotionally, financially, and physically. Words have creative power; whatever you say, then so be it. Before anything can come into fruition, or completion, it has to be thought of first, and then it is usually spoken. Whenever you speak words, it sends messages to the brain to have your body react to what was spoken. Any decent motivational speaker knows this power and will always have you say certain phrases to get you into some sort of positive state. You can try it now. Try telling yourself, "I feel great. I believe in myself, and I will achieve all the goals that I wish to accomplish for myself." If you did it, do it again, this time with more energy and more passion as if you are leading a group of people in this confession.

Notice what happens to your body language. Now say the exact same thing, but this time make sure you are frowning; your head is down, you are sitting down with your shoulder protruded, and your chest is caved in. It feels contrary, doesn't it? Of course it does, because your body is geared to respond openly. You usually smile when you say something good about yourself. Your body will follow your words. Just like on Monday morning—you say "I don't feel like going to work", and if you kept saying that you may not go or your attitude may not be the best that day if you do not change your words.

Everything starts with words. Words and thoughts are the creative force behind everything that was created. It is by words that inventions, books, movies, and plays are created. It is by the words of people that we elect our mayor, senator, or president. Of course there are actions that precede this, but it is by their words that we are compelled to be either for or against them. One presidential candidate withdrew from the race because people misunderstood and misinterpreted his words.

One of my assignments in a business class was to examine my past view of money. As I did that, I began to hear a conversation I used to have with others and myself concerning money. Things like, "I'll never be rich," "The love of money is the root of all evil," and "Money isn't everything." Confessions like that, definitely kept me in poverty. If you are going to be rich, you have to tell yourself that you are. If you say something long enough you will begin to believe it whether it is true or not. I know a woman who doesn't eat watermelon seeds because her mother told her that watermelons would grow in her if she ate them.

To this day she makes sure she carefully removes all the seeds. She knows a watermelon is not going to grow inside her, but that idea is instilled in her.

If you say you are never going to be rich, then you will believe it and that will be your reality. You won't work toward riches because your preconceived values confirm that you will never be rich.

What do you say about yourself?
How about the way you walk, talk, and dress?
Your performance on your job?
Your kids, spouse, and family?

Your brain is like your computer's hard drive; enter positive words and whenever a giant comes to visit you can show him your files of positive phrases and accomplishes. We usually don't give ourselves enough credit for the little things we have accomplished. I have the best mother in the world, but she does not give herself enough credit because of some things she has not accomplished. She has no college education, and she did not complete high school. She raised four children with no support from a man. Yet she managed to purchase a very nice home, invest in funds that increased her finances, and started a day care business. So she is a homeowner, businesswoman, and investor. Most people talk about doing those things; this little Jamaican woman did it.

We have to learn to appreciate and celebrate every success we attain, because when negative words come, there's usually a downpour. There are going to be times when you must power talk to get you through whatever situation comes your way. Power talk prepares you for something greater and confirms what is already in you. Most of the time, we already know the wisdom in the self-help books and tapes we purchased and shows we watched; we just forgot. We need to be reminded in a new way. It has to be presented with a new spin, because we get caught up with bills, kids, relationships and so forth. This poem was inspired by a message that spoke about being already qualified.

Already in Me

I can do anything; yes anything
That I put my heart and mind to do
Because of the many trials and tribulations
I have already gone through
I have already seen amazing strength
And strength comes out of me
Storms that I have already weathered
I've been through high tides and windy seas

You remember how I used to cry
And I swore that I could not last
Who'd ever thought that I'd be telling people
To kill giants in their past
But that's the wonder of God's vast glory
That He allows us to see
That through life's valley, hard times and chaos
He pulls out greatness in me

Sure I've heard it said, you've heard it too
Yes we all have been told
That precious metal must go through fire
In order to be called pure gold
And now I realize the power of words
And the purpose of pain is for me to see
That I must kill my giants
Because giants don't like
The greatness that's already in me

(Written by Jopala Poetry)

*We are what we repeatedly do. Excellence then is
not an act, but a habit.* — Aristotle

The poem cited is a poem of encouragement and reconfirmation. We all have incredible stories of how we made it through difficult times. All of us can verify how during that time we either gave up or felt like giving up and how we could not see the light at the end of the tunnel. In retrospect, we can laugh at some of our past trials. We look back in laughter, because we can hear some of the lame, negative things we were saying and how those things came to pass. Your attitude determines your altitude, and it is also one of the ways you kill your giants. There are people who constantly feel good about themselves because they surround themselves with positive people and words; everything around them produces life.

You've heard the expression that you are what you eat. Well, you are also what you consistently listen to, whom you hang around, and what you see. I am surrounded by people who speak and think highly of me. Before this book was even published, I had people saying, "Write another bestseller," "You're a king," "You're going to be rich," and other empowering statements. They basically said, "Hey, Dave, you're already qualified." You may add to your qualifications through school and other classes but you have what it takes. You are qualified by the gifts that are already in you, and what adds to those qualifications are trials. Your trials are badges of honor.

However, if your mindset is "I always have bad luck; everything bad is happening to me," then you have already missed your blessing. In contrast, consider it pure joy when you face all kind of trials, because the trials work patience, character, and hope (James 1:2. See the difference in paradigms? It is because of abandonment, divorce, and betrayal, to name just a few, that I can write about identifying and killing giants. I don't have to be an expert on human relations to know about human relations. Our trials make us strong and magnify what is already in us.

It takes more energy to be negative than to be positive. Positive words make you feel good and create energy within you. When I compliment women on how they look, it is such a joy to see them smile, relax, and feel good about themselves. Others I have complimented on the delivery of great sermons and their ability to inspire motivation.

I have given compliments to people, and hours later they have thanked me because it boosted their confidence and stayed with them all day.

Here are some advantages of speaking positive words.

1. Healing: Proverbs 15:4 NIV—"The tongue that brings healing is a tree of life.

Kind words are sweet to the soul, they bring life to one's bones." Sometimes, all we need are words of encouragement to change the outlook of a discouraging situation. Right words are sometimes the determining factor between depression and happiness.

2. Encouragement: A few years ago some of my friends and I was unemployed. Shortly thereafter my car engine died. While at times it became depressing, I constantly told myself that I would not let this temporary situation keep me down. I worked on my book and my album, and went back to school. I had to maximize my time and tell myself that brighter days were coming regardless of how I felt. It is important to encourage yourself.

3. Faith: Hebrews 11:1 NIV defines faith perfectly. Faith is being sure of what we hope for and certain of what we do not see.

If you continue to speak positive things to yourself and others, it creates confidence. This also brings an assurance that you can accomplish the goals or dreams that you have. Faith comes by hearing, so what are you listening to? Why not hear your own voice and others telling you that you can achieve whatever it is that you want? You can purchase motivational products from speakers that will inspire you to maximize your potential. This way you can create faith at any point in time.

4. Vision: Proverbs 29:18 NIV — "Where there is no vision, the people cast off restraint."

The great thing about vision is it creates a picture at the beginning with the end in mind. A vision verbalizes what the purpose is and gives you something to work toward. When you speak and write your vision, it reminds you of your goal. Also if you are not around to fulfill the goal others can run with the vision and fulfill your plans. This way you work on leaving a legacy.

Guard Your Door

The doors to your heart are your eyes, ears, and mouth. Out of the abundance of the heart, the mouth speaks (Luke 6:45). This means that the mouth will speak whatever is in the heart. The values that you hold dear to your heart started from a seed. One author said, sow a thought, reap an action; sow an action, reap a habit; sow a set of habits, reap a character; sow a character and reap your destiny. You have to watch what you see and hear, because based on these things you are feeding your inner man what you eat — and you are what you eat.

If faith comes by hearing, then what are you listening to? If you have no faith for your situation, then it is because you are listening to the wrong messages. In order for faith to be revived or even birthed, something has to precede that. That is a message of hope. Faith is the substance of things hoped for and the evidence of things not seen. (Heb. 11:1) Therefore faith and hope are married. How can you have hope without faith? And how can you have faith without hope?

Faith fights against giants because faith rejects hopelessness, which leads to suicide. People contemplate suicide because their passion for life has been choked by life's challenges, and they can't see their circumstances getting any better. Remember that a giant never starts out being a giant; it grows in to one. Therefore it is crucial that we carefully select what we allow to get into us by way of auditory and visual channels.

We don't allow children to watch or listen to just anything because of the possibility of dangerous influences on their minds. Likewise with adults we need to be mindful of what we watch, listen to and say because of the negative impacts it can have on us.

There are people that I've had to cut off from my life because they did not bring me higher. They were coming through my door and producing negativity. They had to be removed. Sometimes it is hard, but nobody is going to guard your door as well as you will. So watch the door of your heart before it gets contaminated

Negative Words Delete

Don't beat yourself up with negative words. There are plenty of people who will stand in line and do that for you. —Kimball Scott

Have you ever been around someone who was always talking negatively about something or someone? Depressing, isn't it? Negativity drains energy and faith, and faith is the substance of dreams coming true. Your words have power; don't allow yourself to continue to say words that don't empower you, but rather allow your words to challenge you. Your words are a key to your success, because they are the foundation of how you think. Words followed by action can change a nation. Get into the habit of using words that help you get the things you need. Proverbs states that an anxious heart weighs a man down, but a kind word cheers him up (Prov. 12:25).

CHAPTER 9

A Time to Kill Giants

There is a time for everything and a season for
every activity under heaven. (Eccl. 3:1)

Number 1: Do It Now

Countless times I have said that I will make that call or attend that meeting, or cancel that appointment, but have failed to do so because I procrastinated. In this fast-paced world where we have so many responsibilities, it is easy to forget important dates and events. As we grow older, our brain cells diminish. While I am only in my early thirties, I am a ship without a sail without my planner.

It is natural for us to forget, and it takes us longer to recall information that was already obtained. Since this is a natural progression, despite all the vitamins and enhancers we take to improve our memory retention, doing things now will help us defeat procrastination. Do not put things off until tomorrow that you can do today. Remember, tomorrow may never come, but when it does, you will continue to say, "I will do it tomorrow." I believe tomorrow is related to someone else.

Do not put things off. Do the things you can accomplish today. Not procrastinating means you are getting things done quicker than others are. I believe those who acquire such an outlook bring themselves closer to their destiny.

Start your goals now! Too many times I have heard people say that they're waiting on some sort of transformation to start certain projects or even to give their life to God. God does not need your help in cleaning up your act before you come to Him. The problem with that is you never know what problems await that would truly deter you from committing your life or getting started. The awesome thing about starting a new project is that it will bring new excitement, and you're already in progress. It may take years before the project is finished, but you are closer than before. Motivational speaker Les Brown said, "You do not have to be great to get started, but you have to get started in order to be great."

I was overwhelmed when I first began writing this book. I had no idea how the process would become a finished product. So many questions were presented. Several months later, things became a lot clearer. Do not make the mistake of not getting started because you don't see how you will finish. Take risks, start now, walk out by faith, and start your dream. That is a powerful way of killing your giants.

Self-Assessment

Because I have been hurt in the past, my tolerance level for some relational issues have decreased. I have a good friend, and our friendship is wonderful but challenging to the point where I felt we should not talk for a season. I went back and forth with the decision on whether to keep the friendship or not, but I didn't want to start a pattern of running away from conflict, so I had to analyze the relationship to determine whether our frequent disagreements were based on mere differences in personality or was it a matter of me shying away from any form of conflict all together. After assessing our friendship and comparing it to others, I felt that this friend would cross the line and offend me too many times. Thus, I began to speak to her more harshly and at times abruptly even in ordinary conversation. She realized she could deal with me, but I could not reciprocate. I found her to be very high-maintenance, loud, and domineering, traits that do not compliment my boisterous, upfront and frank personality. While we maintained the friendship, we decided to decrease the amount of time we spoke in order to carry on a relatively amicable relationship.

The best way to soothe my temper is by using soft words. If you bite me with harshness, I'm probably going to return the favor. A gentle answer calms me down. I find it difficult to even raise my voice to a woman with a gentle, warm voice. What works for me may not work for others. You have to be honest with yourself. When you realize what you can and cannot tolerate, it deletes unnecessary drama in your relationships. Do not waste someone else's time if you don't know what you want. I have witnessed other relationships end because both people finally came to the conclusion that the other person was not what they really wanted from the beginning. We take people through unnecessary trials because we do not spend enough time by ourselves trying to find out what our likes and dislikes are. Some may argue and say that you really don't know until you experience some things. My reply to that is that experience may be the best teacher, but only fools attend that school!

Write down what makes you angry. One of the frustrations men experience with women is that they believe women do not know what they want. The nerve right? Men complain that women want to be loved and romanced. When men express this, women still complain. One of the problems is that men will perform their mission of love and romance only to experience a letdown, because the woman did not specify how she wanted to receive love. In their defense, men are not mind readers. I have heard women say that they should not have to tell men about the specifics—how they feel and so forth. That's why communication is an essential tool. A piece of advice to women would be instead of faking your orgasms, tell and teach him what you want and how to achieve that goal. His ego may be deflated for a time, but once he understands it, it becomes a win-win situation, and you will be grateful to each other later.

Be Honest with Yourself

I had the most interesting night when I was working an overnight shift. I was working at the front desk of a hotel, and the line was short. As I was checking in a party of four guests, there was an interracial couple behind them. I periodically looked at the woman waiting behind my guests thinking a few different thoughts. At first she appeared to be very happy with him, but they did not look like a "couple." I assumed it was probably just a sex thing for the night. The second thought was that she was a fairly attractive white woman who seemed to be educated and intelligent. Why was she with this...thug?

Prior to her coming to the counter, I was having a conversation with my coworker about black people who act inappropriately and speak in urban slang in the hotel. The conversation lasted just a few minutes as I concluded checking in one of my guests. When she finally approached the counter, she gave me her identification for check-in and asked me how I was doing. I responded that I was well. When I looked at her driver's license and asked her if anyone has ever mentioned that she resembled a particular recording artist. She responded "yes, it had been mentioned, but she was a lot classier."

Her date saw someone he knew and began to speak to them. After the third word, I looked at him and thought "this is exactly what I was talking about, the thuggish behavior." I saw her response to his slang; she looked totally disgusted. I did not reply, but my face asked, "Why are you with him?" She verbally answered, "Don't even ask." At this point, he went outside to park the car. As I was making a copy of her ID, I was amazed at how much we were communicating without speaking a word. Since I wasn't sure what her previous look meant, I decided to slip my business card between her credit card and ID. As I gave her back her cards, she noticed my card and asked, "What is this?" I felt horrible and embarrassed. She responded professionally by smiling and said, "Have a good night."

A few minutes later, she walked back in by herself and I took that opportunity to apologize. While my motive was only to talk and figure out why she was with him, I knew I was wrong. I was dumbfounded for about thirty minutes and had to ask myself what was going on inside of me. One thing I noticed was that in the past when I was lonely, my flirting techniques increased by 70 percent. Not only did I flirt with her but I also flirted with the guest before her. To add insult to injury, both women were with their men, which is a high form of disrespect. While that was not something that I normally did, I realized that I had to constantly assess myself to determine why I was doing what I was doing. If we learn to ask that questions before and during our actions, we will not only be surprised at the answers but we will be able to change them.

The Strongest Link

Three months after my separation from my ex-wife, I entered into another relationship. I thought this woman was everything I wanted and needed. The relationship lasted two months and was filled with intensity on every level. After that relationship ended, there was a great void, and I tried to fill it through personal achievements and sporadic dating. Every woman I met or dated thereafter I would compare to her, and they failed miserably. I missed her, and it was more frustrating because I could not get her off my mind.

After speaking with my mentor, I realized that no one would ever compare to her and that no woman would ever come close to making me feel the way this women did- not because she was a goddess-like, perfect woman, but because of the circumstances when I met her. At the time I was broken, vulnerable, and needy and she supplied a lot of my needs when my state of mind was frail. The decisions I made then were not sound or wise. I am a lot stronger, wiser, and more level-headed now. My standards are higher now, and it's going to take a lot more to impress me.

We have to be careful that the associations we create are not counterfeit, because we are in desperate need. One of the worst things anyone can do is attach oneself to a relationship based on a rebound. That person may act like your savior because you're meeting him or her at a vulnerable stage of your life. Since time has a way of healing wounds, you tend to start seeing things more clearly with the passage of time. In time, I realized that everything that glittered was not gold. I began to realize that she too was using me to fill certain voids in her life. I concluded that we were no good for each other and the relationship ended.

A link is simply created by memory. For instance, every time you hear a certain love song, it brings a certain person to mind. Christmastime for some means shopping and presents. Your strongest link will depend on what you are going through at that time.

One of my strongest links was after a performance of one of my songs. The crowd was hyped and filled with joy. They were in awe. People were clapping and praising God. As I was walking back, a man who knew me pulled me aside and hugged me. He would not let me go. The song blessed him so much that he had tears streaming down his face. He continued to hold me and thank me. His friend had to pull him away. That moment has surpassed every compliment, scream, and encouragement because of the way it affected him.

The links we have are both positive and negative... For the ones that are negative, we have to reprogram our minds and thoughts. New thoughts can change how the old links made us feel. Sometimes it is as simple as a new hobby or toy. However, this may be a process where you must go back and rethink why, when, and how. While this may be taxing at times, look at the end result. You will feel liberated— a brand-new you. A healthier paradigm and another giant tossed in the fire, destroyed forever.

Can You Hear Me Now?

How many times did you go through unnecessary drama because you did not listen to the wisdom of your spouse, friends, or parents? The decisions we make today impact our tomorrow. Often the turmoil we find ourselves in is our own fault, because we make stupid decisions. Many of us choose to live for the moment, without thinking of the repercussions. A good friend of mine as a teenager was warned publicly through a prophecy to stop playing games and get his life together. He was told that God had a calling on his life.

He was always attracted to the streets and tried to find satisfaction there. One of his wakeup calls was that he was stabbed at a party. It just so happened that there was a nurse on the scene who helped him, and that provided a quicker recovery period. Shortly thereafter, he moved out of state to get away from the city life. The streets called him again, and he answered the call unfavorably. This time he, along with another friend of mine, committed assault and battery, and he is currently doing time.

Another friend was called to preach and had incredible potential. He even spoke to me about his dreams, which was so inspiring because he had so much passion. I will never forget the moment when I received a phone call from his ex-wife stating that he died from a drug overdose. I was so angry with God. I questioned God. What happened to the prophecy? Was this man of God wrong? God's answer was "I have been calling them for years. I have been knocking for years, but he would not answer."

He is knocking at your door, but will you answer? Please do not get to your wit's end trying to figure things out before you give Him your attention. I urge you not to let a tragedy enter your life before you heed His call. Don't let allow sin to deafen the voice of God. It would be sad to get so caught up in what you're doing that you cannot hear the voice of destiny. While God is merciful, He will not be made a fool. Do not think that because He is loving and full of grace that He will not turn away from your disaster.

Time is not always on our side. People often say, "I'll give my life tomorrow" or "I'm waiting for something special to happen." But you really don't know what is going to happen tomorrow. That is not said to scare you, but it is a hard truth. While we make plans for our future, our steps are often ordered. Proverbs 20:24 says "A man's steps are directed by the Lord. How then can anyone understand his own way?" You cannot always understand your own way, because you are not in total control. There are reasons why you meet the people you do and go the places you go: your purpose. There is something that God wants you to do. Don't let a tragedy enter your life in order to do what is right. He's calling you. He's saying, "Can you hear me? Can you hear me now?"

Whom Do You Hang With?

If you want to soar like eagles, why are you hanging with ducks? The people you spend time with are a representation of who you are. If you're the kind of person who thinks life is about fun and good times and your actions display that continuously, then the time I spend with you has to be limited. If you are a television or movie buff, the same applies. Many times I would say, "It's just a waste of precious time." The people I spend most of my time with, are the people who share a similar mind set as I do and are goal orientated. If you want to be great, link yourself with people who are great or at least who are on that path.

People have criticized NBA Coach Phil Jackson of the L.A. Lakers because he went from one championship team to another. The argument was of course that L.A. was going to win another championship. Look at the team. There is a difference between working hard and working smart. If you can have sweat-less victories in less time, then obtain them. My children will not have to work as hard as I did, because there is a path that I am preparing for them. I have a music producer who elevates my musical intelligence and my songs. He makes me sound better because of his expertise. If you associate with excellence, it will become you. In the same way, if you associate yourself with poverty or laziness, that will also rub off on you. Often you do not have the same mindset as others do, but if you're with them, you can receive the same blessing or punishment.

How about the young man who was arrested because he did not know his friends had drugs in the car? How about the wife who cannot reach her goals because she has a controlling husband? What about the husband who feels like less of a man because his wife is condescending due to his meager salary? My friend was shot and killed because he was at a party. Wrong place, wrong time, and wrong company. I believe that if I had stayed with some of the people from my past, this book would not have been written because they did not have my best interest at heart.

The people you surround yourself with should be like-minded or on a higher level than you. There should be something about them that inspires or challenges you. They should also bring out the best in you, which could be you being a mentor or you being mentored. The people who can take you to the next level are the ones you should associate with. You need to link up with people who have the highest regard for you and share your passion as well as feel your pain. Delete all "fair-weather" friends. Remember, the company you keep is a representation of who you are.

CHAPTER 10

Battle of the Exes

OK guys, class has now begun, and today we're going to talk about baby mama drama. "Hey, hey, pick me!" David says. "Make sure we don't forget about the ladies, and baby daddy drama," one woman said.

I think one of the frustrating things a person has to deal with is the fact that they must communicate with the person they broke up with or divorced because they have a child together. If the breakup was bitter, then communication is usually not pleasant.

The hostility between the two parties is often expressed in the most disrespectful way, for several reasons. One, the seed of rejection has now been watered and it's never pleasant being rejected by someone with whom you had a relationship. Nobody wants to be told all the negative reasons why it can't work out or the only way that he or she can retain sanity is to leave you. The process of rejection can either make you bitter or better. During these times some people find strength to encourage themselves. That is why songs like "I Will Survive," "Survivor," "Looking for a New Love" and "I'll Get Over You" were written. They are a part of our medicine; for others it may be something else or a combination of several things such as staying busy, working more, hanging with friends or entering new relationships.

It is natural to feel angry with the one that you are separated from, because you feel this person is responsible for your current negative emotions. While it is OK to be temporarily angry, the important question is how that anger is channeled. It is not good when anger is allowed to come to a boil or when you allow yourself to get so angry that you act out of character. It is vital to recognize that there are some issues that will arise when talking to your ex, even when you are talking about the child or children. In order to keep things in perspective, you must set some ground rules.

Ground Rule Number 1: You're in Control

Your ex knows exactly how to push your buttons; they are aware of what sneaky remarks are going to set you off. Too many times I have allowed myself to be upset hours after a conversation with my ex, only to realize later that I gave more energy to the argument than it was worth. Say goodbye to the attitudes that arise, which work against you. As corny as it may sound, if you picture each negative emotion that surfaces when dealing with your wonderful ex and you see yourself saying goodbye to it, this process actually helps delete old associations and create new ones. Motivational speakers will tell you to first picture victory in your mind. The mind is the first and last place of battle; it is where the war is won or lost. If you can't see yourself in control and winning, then it makes no sense gearing up for battle.

Ground Rule Number 2:
You're Not with Him or Her Anymore

Why do you get so caught up with what your ex says anyway? The caring factor definitely goes down a lot because...umm...let me think... oh yeah, you're my ex. You cannot and should not allow your ex to have the same influence on you as they did when you were together. Otherwise, you would never have broken up. Be careful not to let them play mind games on you because they know your weaknesses.

You must constantly ask yourself why you respond this way.

How much do you care and why?

Do you still love him or her? Why?

Are you over him or her?

Be honest when you are answering these questions; the answers will be a guide in letting you know why you do, what you do concerning your previous relationship. Since you're not with him anymore, stop giving him advice. Even if there is sound wisdom and doctrine in what you are saying, the last person he wants to receive rebuke or correction from is you, because there is too much animosity between the two of you.

It baffles me to see couples who are not together anymore trying to tell each other what is wrong and right. I believe you are wasting precious energy, because if he barely listened to you when you were with him, what makes you think he is going to listen to you now? Stop reminding her about the old patterns that bring current frustrations to the relationship. It is beyond a matter of pride; it is a matter of position. Since you are not the main squeeze in her life, you now lose credibility. The question is not whether you're right or wrong; it is the stigma of the relationship. It is futile to think you have the same influence or authority you did when you were together.

Ground Rule Number 3: Demand Respect

After a while, the cold, abrupt, and disrespectful conversations become draining and old. With anything in life, you must become sick and tired of being sick and tired. If you are experiencing too many distasteful conversations, tell your ex, "If you can't talk to me in a decent manner over the phone, I will hang up, and you will have to leave a voicemail. And if that is disrespectful, it will be like I never got the call because as soon as I hear distaste, I will press delete." Either one of two things will happen. One, he or she is going to get tired of being hung up on or he or she will change their tone. I am not saying that it will be that easy or that this will work for everyone; your situation is unique. However, something has to be done and said in order for dialogue to be received and given in a respectful manner.

Ground Rule Number 4: Closure

One true way to experience peace of mind is to obtain closure. Where there is no closure, there will be restlessness. There has always been a sense of incompleteness, because I never met my father. After years of yearning to see him, to experience at least what he looks like and to understand his personality, I began to lose hope and became numb to certain facts. The fact may be that I will never see my father and hear his voice. I may never understand from his point of view why he couldn't stay in his son's life and be daddy to me.

It may be similar in that you and your ex never talked about why you broke up and what really went wrong. A lot of people, including myself, feel incomplete because there were so many things we wanted to say but never got the chance to say. Many times we don't get closure and feel robbed, because we feel a part of our life is stagnant. It is essential to get closure, because it provides security and completion. However, an important point to remember here is that we create the rules. God forbid you never get closure in certain relationships; this does not mean you can't move on. What it does mean is that you formulate your own conversations that empower you to say, "I'm OK now." Even though I never knew my father, this does not mean that I cannot be a good father. Even though my first marriage did not work, does not mean my present one won't. Notice the past two statements focused on future goals and not on a muddy past. You see, you can create your own closure and end internal turmoil on a note that empowers you and makes you feel more in control.. Winners are the ones who adapt to their situations and create whole new ones.

Ground Rule Number 5: Stop Hooking Up

If you want him to take you seriously, then stop sleeping with him. (sorry, guys). Ladies, unfortunately most men are not going to turn down a bootie call. You diminish your authority and respect (the little that you have, because of your position) when you do this. This also brings confusion into the broken relationship because both of you are probably on two different courses. His course could be, "I am in emotional pain so I need sexual pleasure and physical relief," and it ends there. Your course could be, "Well, he is my baby's father, and maybe there is a chance we can still be together; there is a part of me that will always love him. He knows I would not give my body to just anybody, so why is he treating me like this?" Whoa, put the car in park and let's talk this over. Please understand that my motive is not to put women in a weak state of mind with this example. However, there are many times when I have seen women willing to compromise because of a child connection instead of mutual love. As harsh as this may sound, mutual love has to be the only determining factor in whether you would consider getting back with him. The fact that you have a child with him has nothing to do with the equation of sleeping with him or reestablishing a relationship with him.

Too many couples stay or get back together because of the children. Nobody is really happy, because you two are living a lie; sooner or later, the children will see it. Another reason for not sleeping with each other anymore is that it keeps your emotions and habits intact and consistent. It deletes confusion, maintains or enhances respect, and keeps the gateway of communication honest. Sleeping with someone is not just an act of physical expression. There are emotions that get involved; that is only natural. If you don't want your communication to be further misconstrued, stop hooking up.

CHAPTER 11

The Spiritual Factor

All scripture is God breathed and is useful for teaching, rebuking, correcting and training in righteousness, so that the man of God may be thoroughly equipped for every good work.
(2 Tim. 3:16 NIV)

What goes into the mind and body comes out. The things you see and hear are up to you. Thank God I was never deeply into pornography, but there was a short season when I watched pornographic videos. During that time, I had the wildest lustful dreams. For the untrained spirit this may have been OK, but for me it felt like an unnatural evil weight trying to attach itself to me. Not only did I stop watching such videos, but I destroyed them.

We are people made of flesh, soul, and spirit. The spirit is the inner core of a man's heart and mind.

The spirit is the part of the person that can respond to God. There is not a material substance to the spirit. It needs a place to breathe. There is one spirit inside of a person but many spirits can attach themselves to it. Mark 5 tells of a story about a man who was possessed by an evil spirit. His behavior was so violent, that he had to be held in chains, which he often broke. Literally no one could calm him down. He lived in tombs and caves and would cut himself with stones and cry out both day and night. When he saw Jesus, the spirit shrieked and said, "What do you want with me?" Jesus then ordered the spirit to come out. He asked, "What is your name"? The spirit responded, "Legion, for we are many."

A Roman legion was made up of six thousand men. While the Scriptures do not say exactly how many demons had possessed this man, it is obvious that there were many, based on his behavior. A spirit needs a place to be housed. It is up to you to decide which ones to house. Giants can be spirits; the spirit is what makes the man. Let me make this clear: We are not demon-possessed because we have negative attitudes, but keep in mind that the devil does linger around seeking a door where he can gain entrance to you. Furthermore, when the enemy comes, he is not blatantly intrusive; he approaches with small cunning steps that actually lead to a massive downfall. For example, the alcoholic does not take his first drink saying that he is going to be addicted to alcohol.

We all have done and said some things we thought we would never do or say. Think about it: What was going on with you at the time? How did you get into that frame of mind? How did it start, and how did it progress? How does it start with the rapist, the pedophile, or the serial killer? Something happened somewhere when the cynical behaviors were introduced. It bears repeating: a giant never starts out as being a giant; it grows into one. The mind is the central place where spirits are influenced; it is where every battle is lost or won. Most importantly, it is where the battles starts and finishes. Romans 12:2 states "Don't copy the behavior and customs of this world, but let God transform you into a new person by changing the way you think. Then you will know what God wants you to do, and you will know how good and pleasing and perfect his will really is (Rom. 12:2 NLT).

We live in a society of do what you want, how you want, when you want, and as long as you want, so long as you are not hurting anyone and you feel good. Wow, can you see all the giants in those statements? Our nation has removed prayer from schools, wants to take God out of the Pledge of Allegiance, advocates the removal of the Ten Commandments from public buildings, and even challenges the phrase "In God we trust" on our currency. It also supports taking Christ out of Christmas and just saying "Happy Holidays" because we don't want to offend anyone. What about offending Christians and Christ?

Yet when tragedy hits, we want God back in our nation again. We treat Him like a food item that we have eliminated from our diet. So many people blame God because they do not understand tragedy. They ask, "Well, if God is so merciful, why did He let this person die? And why does He allow people to commit such hideous crimes?" It's because He loves us so much that He wanted to give us choice. That is what the American way is all about—the power to choose. He already has angels that do nothing but worship and praise Him.

People choose to do good just as they choose to do evil. But while people are blaming God for the bad things that happen, they do not seem to recognize that there is a devil and that he is not this little red guy with pointy ears and a red cloak. One of the most powerful statements I've heard is that one of the things that the devil has done is convince people that he is not real. It seems as if he has done an excellent job. Second Corinthians 4:4 reads, "The god of this age has blinded the minds of unbelievers, so that they cannot see the light of the gospel of the glory of Christ, who is the image of God (2 Cor 4:4 NIV)." The god of this age—notice the small "g"—is the devil, who is the enemy of God. It is not surprising that we do not hold him accountable for the horrible things that happen. Imagine all the crimes you could commit if nobody could identify you because you were invisible and therefore people thought you were a myth.

People are so comfortable doing whatever they want with no regard to future repercussions. For every action, there is a reaction, and sometimes it will be a chain reaction. A lot of people do not want to convert to Christianity because of the things they will not be able to do afterwards. What they don't keep in mind are the things they will not be able to do, are not good for them anyway. God does not set rules in order to punish us; they are there to protect us. Sin is fun, and the devil is going to make it extremely attractive, but the end is a path of destruction.

When we don't do things God's way, we end up with cities and nations that are in chaos and in desperate need of help, and all the psychologists, counselors, marriage experts, and twelve-step programs can only help so much. Ephesians 6:10-12 says, "Finally, be strong with the Lord's mighty power. Put on all of God's armor so that you will be able to stand firm against all strategies and tricks of the Devil. For we are not fighting against people made of flesh and blood, but against the evil rulers and authorities of the unseen world, against those mighty powers of darkness who rule this world, and against wicked spirits in the heavenly realms" Eph. 6:10-12 NLT).

You cannot win a spiritual battle using human intellect. The devil is called the father of lies; he is a deceiver. He deceived Eve into eating the fruit; he deceived David into sleeping with Bathsheba. He deceived Samson into sleeping with Delilah and telling her the secret of his strength and he deceived Isaac into thinking that he was giving Esau his blessing instead of Jacob. Trust me, the devil is real, and he is not on your side. He only comes to steal, kill and destroy your destiny. If you are going to blame anyone for giants, he is an awesome place to start. Just like God has a nature, the devil has a nature, and it is your responsibility to find out whose nature is blessing or cursing you.

A giant can easily be a curse, especially in generations. Do you really think it is a coincidence that your grandfather and father were alcoholics and now you are? Poverty is a curse and a giant. Dysfunctional homes are a curse and a giant. There are many more I could list, but I think you get the idea. Break the curse; kill the giants.

God often does things that do not make sense, but if you understand how He operates you know He does that to let you know He is in control and you had nothing do with the blessing or miracle that took place. Otherwise, you would give yourself the credit. But when you know without a shadow of a doubt that God intervened in your situation, it releases your faith and confirms His power. The problem with many people is that they do not see God as one they can talk to and bring their problems to. Instead they make negative assumptions about Him, especially when the storms of life overtake them.

The bigger picture is what you can do as a Christian not what you can't do. God wants to put His super on your natural, and when He does, it will exceed your dreams if you stay in Him. Most people do not understand God because they do not spend time with Him through prayer and reading the Bible. They try to figure Him out with their understanding and when they can't they get frustrated and decide to do things their way. How foolish is it for anyone to try to figure out the almighty God! Common sense should tell you that His ways far surpass our ways and thoughts. But as Mark Twain said, "common sense is very uncommon." God is inexhaustible and sovereign; He is the Alpha and the Omega, the beginning and the end and a whole lot more. You cannot figure out God because He is God—and the day you do, you would become equal to Him. If you knew all His ways, then His position would no longer be superior.

It is not God's responsibility to conform to you; it is your responsibility to conform to Him because He is God. It is a matter of honor, respect, and position. When certain people step into my presence, I stand; if an elderly person or pregnant woman needs a seat on the bus or train, I will offer mine. I am a grown man, but I still watch my tone with my mother no matter how upset she makes me. It is a matter of position (plus she will knock me out). Based on one's position, a certain respect is due them. It is the same with God; it does not change because you cannot see Him.

People claim they do not believe in God or have a problem with faith, but people use their faith every day. When you put your kids on the school bus, you believe you will see them later that day. When you travel by car or train, you believe you will get to your destination safely. When you board a plane, you do not ask the pilot how many times he has done this. When you sit on a chair, do you check the legs to see if it will hold you up? Tomorrow is not promised to any of us; yet we all have plans for the future—or at least a day planner. These are examples of faith being exercised; it's just a matter of channeling it to the right source.

There is so much power in believing. This book is primarily about believing in yourself to achieve a great destiny by removing anything that will keep you from it, on any level. You don't have to have millions of dollars or be famous to achieve greatness. To have anything or do anything great, you must believe. If you look throughout the Bible, especially in the New Testament, you will see that the greatest sin is not murder, slander, adultery, or drunkenness— to name a few: it is unbelief. As a matter of fact, the greatest sins committed by our forefathers in the Bible were they did not believe God would do what He said He would do. In our spiritual walk with God, if we truly believed we would not disobey.

Destiny and greatness will always be cut short, if you do not believe. Some people say they are Christians but they don't know what that means, because Christian means Christ-like. What kills me are the artists who praise themselves on their records and talk about sex, money, power, and bling-bling, and then when they get an award they say, "First and foremost, I would like to thank Jesus Christ my Lord and Savior." At that point I am screaming at the TV saying, "What Lord?" If He is Lord, it means that He controls you by His Spirit—what you say, the music you put out, the motives behind what you do are in line with His Word, which is the Bible. Do not say something just because it sounds spiritual or people like to hear it.

God loves us and has a wonderful plan for our lives. He has shown some of that by the talents He has placed in us. The thing you naturally do well is a gift from God, but He will not force Himself on us. He will be as awesome as you allow Him to be. Ephesians 3:20 says, "Now unto him who is able to do exceedingly abundantly above all we ask or think, according to the power that is at work within us".

Confessions of Faith

Remember that faith is the substance of things hoped for, the evidence of things not seen (see Heb. 11:1 NKJV). No one hopes for what he already has, which means it is the unseen things (things we desire to have) we believe we will attain. A good motivational speaker will tell you that a positive confession is key to success, because it releases faith and conditions your mind for success. Many successful businessmen speak positive confessions every day, sometimes two to three times daily. They believe that by speaking positive words they become empowered in their subconscious minds. Therefore, by doing these things every day, they form habits of success. You can either copy someone else's confession or make up your own. What matters is that something more is being done to kill your giants.

Please note that if you see successful people and different authors saying the same thing, put it into practice. The reason people are successful is because they have been observing and emulating others. Let's put this into practice immediately. For example say aloud:

❏ "I will not succumb to inconsistency because it produces mediocrity, and I am above average."
❏ "I will conquer laziness, because laziness produces poverty."

❏ "I am rich in faith, love, patience, and joy, and I will create an effective plan to achieve things in abundance."

❏ "I currently have enough knowledge to create multiple streams of wealth."

❏ "Success will come to me naturally on every level, because I am a man/woman of diligence."

❏ "I will increase in knowledge so that I can obtain all that God has for me."

❏ "I am a winner, regardless of my current situation and feeling. I am not ruled by emotions. I am a man/woman of principles."

And the list could go on. I say different confessions; some vary, depending on what I am going through, and others are consistent. Your yesterdays do not determine your todays, and your today does not determine your tomorrow. The most important confession you can and will ever make is the one where you make Jesus Christ the Lord over your life. This is a prayer seeking forgiveness, which you can confess anywhere, if it is from the heart. Jesus loves you, and He died so you might be free. Your destiny in Him is amazing, so why don't you just say that prayer now?

"Lord Jesus, I confess that I am a sinner. But today I am turning away from my old ways, and I am inviting You into my heart. I ask that You would forgive me for all my sins. I believe God raised Jesus from the dead for my sins, and I declare right now by faith that I am saved. Thank You, Jesus, for saving me."

If that was your first time saying that, praise God, and if you meant it, you really are saved. There are angels in heaven rejoicing over you right now. You should tell a few of your supportive friends. This was a very important and wise decision. Please follow up by attending a solid church, one that preaches the Word of God. Pray and ask God for friends who will help you on your Christian journey.

A very good friend of mine wrote the following poem. It explains my yesterdays, today's, and tomorrows.

Established

My Lord, My Salvation, My Savior,
As I walk in a place of despair and defeat,
You saved me from darkness and brought me to
    Your light,
From blindness to vision and sight.

But I stumble still as I try to do Your will,
Fall back to my blindness out of Your
    alignment.
Forgetting my deliverance I embrace the lie,
Suddenly, crash! The pain and sorrow begins,
Your Holy Spirit begins the surgery, uncovering
    my sins.

No longer kept hidden now brought to light,
I run to Your altar of immeasurable grace,
My tears on Your throne You begin to wipe
my face.

Confessed, repented and delivered,
My Father came and set this captive free, that
    was me!
I can now see the truth that's been revealed,
My mind once tainted now made whole and
    clean,
Renewing of my mind made visible seen.

Let the doorways of my heart be heavenly
    guarded,
As all, which entangles has now been discarded.
Place Your truth in the inner part,
Create in me a pure and clean heart.

No longer confusion, rejection or fear,
You begin to pour and fill me with
Your peace,
As You whisper, "I am precious and dear".
Reaffirming that we will never be apart,
And how You will always be near to my heart.

I am blessed! The mask is removed.
The masquerade and façade is no longer intact,
You now have free reign, come in to my heart.
Let Your vision of who I am in You increase,
I walk in Your splendor, Your power released.

Confident in holiness vindicated by Your blood,
Healed by Your power, delivered by Your love.
I am given a new name, no longer the same,
A mass of clay, I am not!

No longer formless without purpose or care,
I am a child of God, an heir.
You created a vessel of strength,
Filled with Your presence, with purpose in
    mind,
I am stamped! Delivered and signed!

Praise be to my Lord, I am cleansed and made
    whole,
Embracing in fullness, Living Waters for
my soul.
I am a gift of God, justified by faith,
I now walk in His boldness as my Lord sets
the pace.

No longer in bondage from my hurts and pains,
Your presence accessible to reign.
My giants, now my triumphs,
Not a victim but a conqueror.
Validated by My Lord, received not rejected,
My weakness is now my strength perfected.

The Holy Spirit in me invested,
I walk empowered as my destiny is revealed.
To be all I was intended, no longer a wish
    concealed.
As He begins to replace in me all that was lost,
I shout a joy of praise as all my giants are
    tossed!

Broken, molded, and refined,
He says to me, "Go and conquer all that is
    ordained to be Mine!

Written by Kareen Casey/
Inspired by Kill Your Giants

CHAPTER 12

A Few More Things

*What comes out of a man is what makes him
unclean. For from within, out of men's hearts,
comes evil thoughts, sexual immorality, theft,
murder, adultery, greed, malice, deceit lewdness,
envy, slander, arrogance and folly. All these evils
come from inside and make a man unclean.*
(Mark 7:20-23 NIV)

Abuse Not Thy Power

Women know if they play their cards right,
they can get anything they want from a man.
They know that men are visual and full of ego. So
they know exactly how to stimulate his emotions to
cater to their desires. In the same way, men know if
we cater to a woman's emotions, we can get what
we want. We've heard that men are not sensitive,
and that we don't talk to women enough, we don't

engage in enough foreplay, flowers, blah, blah, blah (just kidding). Since we know that women like to be treated like queens and men want to be treated like kings, let's not play games with each other for selfish ambition. Men, don't lead women on just because you know you have the skills to woo them. Women, don't entice men with your provocative style just because men are visual and are naturally sexual. There are way too many guessing games that adults play with each other, and some people are proud of how they are able to swindle a man of his money and a woman of her mind and her heart. These are deadly games, and people have gotten hurt physically and emotionally by them.

While I have never hit a woman, I know how it feels to want to physically punish one because she has broken me down and made me feel like less than a man. Women seem to forget that men are physical by nature, and so when a man feels as if he has been broken down, his first response is to conquer. Not every man is going to conquer by verbally communicating, which leaves only a few options. The sad thing is that not all men have the self-control to keep from being violent against a woman when they have been hurt. Relationships are a very tender area so be careful and monitor your motives.

I look forward to a day when domestic violence is at an all-time low across the nation. I wish divorce were not an option in relationships, because people were marrying for love and were determined to honor their vows, instead of the demands of their emotions and their careers. I pray that people would value morals over the power of choice and that sex would be a sacred expression between a husband and a wife. Choice comes with freedom, and freedom is wonderful when it is not abused. We have all been given freedom and power. There is a freedom to choose between right and wrong and the power to act accordingly.

Parents have a lot of power in that their children are submitted to their ways, values, and standards. Parents, lead the way by example and say, "OK, follow me." The most influential parent is the one that can say, "Do as I do and not just what I say." The parent who says, "do what I say" can be viewed as a hypocrite. It is one thing for a parent to tell a child to read and clean; it's another for the child to see them reading and cleaning. What this does in the mind of the child is produce a higher level of respect, because it's not just words; they are seeing your actions. This lets them know that you are not abusing your power. A child is more likely to look up to you when he sees you living what you are preaching.

A Parent's Apology

The first person a woman gives her heart to is her father and the first person to break her heart is her father. —Jackie Williams

We as parents sometimes produce a picture to our children that we are flawless. Nothing could be further from the truth. When we tell our children some of our weaknesses, it reassures them, they are OK.

I had the pleasure of seeing eight children honor their father. What was most memorable for me that night was a son giving a speech about how his nationally known father, apologized to him for mistreating him one day. It changed his whole perspective on his father and increased the respect he had for him because it showed humility. When we apologize to our children for mistreating them, it empowers them emotionally; it raises their self-esteem, strengthens the relationship, and provides security. When you sincerely say you're sorry, it is an expression of love and appreciation, and it states that you will not abuse them or take the relationship for granted. However, the words "I am sorry" are not passwords for you to do the same thing over and over. It means to repent, which means to turn around or to change. A sincere apology from a parent provides security and increases value in the parent-child relationship. It also teaches children to admit when they are wrong, because children often emulate what they see.

Be a Man or Woman of Your Word

There used to be a time when a business transaction was secured by a handshake. Now we need a twenty- page contract, and there is still confusion because of misread loopholes. We need to be the kind of people whose word is our bond. You should be a person who is dependable and reliable. The only thing you have is your word. If people can't depend on that, then what can they rely on? Follow through and keep your commitments and appointments. My kids know if I say that I will take them to dinner on Friday, then on Friday they can expect to go out to dinner. However, if I always canceled our plans, then this would paint a picture in their minds that Daddy is not reliable, and they won't trust what I say. Anytime you let someone know you will do something for him or her, it sets up a mental expectation or excitement, depending on what it is. Therefore, if you do not come through, it can speak volumes to the recipient. Of course, there will be emergencies that will arise, and plans will be altered. In times like these, please call. Nobody wants to be stood up. Your word is your bond; stick to it, even when it hurts.

Motives

Who wants to marry a millionaire? Of course you do; so do I. When I viewed that show on TV I had a few choice words for the contestants. While I definitely understand a woman's need for financial security, some have taken this too far. If money becomes your primary motive instead of love, then you are asking for trouble. We all have seen too many relationships, and marriages crumble because people have wrong motives. While your victim may not know your true intentions, time has a potent way of bringing things to light. Furthermore, before warned that whatever you sow is what you will reap, and it usually comes back at least twice as hard as you gave it. Your motives are important because they show why you do what you do. There are certain blessings you can receive only if your motives are right.

The Power of Belief

Never underestimate the power of belief. If there is anything that crushes a dream, it's unbelief. Your actions will always confirm whether you really believe in something. Maybe it's a job that you need to pursue, but you have been procrastinating, and the reason you're delaying the process is that you are concerned about whether you will succeed at it. It is unbelief that causes some man to walk away from his responsibility as a father and not be involved in the lives of his children. There may be an unbelief that he can't provide an adequate lifestyle for them or spend the kind of quality time he needs to because of his current situation. Therefore he takes an all-or-nothing approach to his kids. It is unbelief that causes couples to throw in the towel with regard to their marriage, believing that divorce is the only or the better option instead of fighting to create new and healthier ways to love each other. It was unbelief that caused Peter to take his eyes off Jesus and put them on the stormy seas, thereby causing him to sink.

I could continue, but I believe you get the point. The giant of unbelief is at the core of a lot of unfulfilled dreams. Unbelief steals the zeal away from life and purpose. The power to act and believe is what separates the men from the boys and the women from the girls. To believe is to simply have faith in something that has not yet come to pass. The action of belief will mean the difference between a mediocre marriage and a wonderful one or one in which you are just going through the motions. For some of us it is the difference between a five, six- or eight-figure annual salaries. Don't let it be said of you that the reason you are not living up to your full potential is that you don't believe. We must think big; we have enough small thinkers in the world. I admit, thinking big is a very scary thing at first. But the unknown for a lot of us is often scary. However, it is the unfamiliar territory that will take us to extraordinary heights. Les Brown said, it not that we think too high and miss it, but rather that we think too low and hit it. As a man thinks in his heart, so is he, so think big dreams and pursue them with vigilance.

CHAPTER 13

The Cost of Not Killing Them

A man who remains stiff-necked after many rebukes
will suddenly be destroyed without remedy.
(Prov. 29:1 NLT)

I was eighteen years old and in a mental institution for the sixth time. Teenagers with similar mental disorders surrounded me. I grew close to two of the patients there. One was Carl and the other was Lisa. Occasionally, if we exhibited good behavior, the staff would let us have passes for the weekend to see our parents. Carl and I talked a lot about many different things. We became very close in a short amount of time; we lived together and had a lot in common. One day he said something to Lisa and I that disturbed me. He stated that after Lisa and I were discharged, he didn't know how he was going to make it. We both assured him that he would be fine, plus we would all keep in touch with each other after we left.

A mental institution can feel like a mini prison. Because patients wanted to get weekend passes, we performed little tricks such as cheating on our medication, and acted as if we were mentally stable, even though we were not. This is where Oscar performances were truly birthed. I decided to follow suit, because I got tired of some doctor telling me I was not ready or mentally stable to see my family. Therefore, I lied about my mental state and behaved exceptionally well. As a result, they granted me a pass, and to go home for the weekend and I was elated. During that weekend, I had a terrible fight with my mother. We argued for the whole time and almost got into a fist-fight because I was not mentally stable.

Upon my return to the hospital, I was eager to see Carl, so I asked the staff where he was. They paused and told me to sit down. They told me that over the weekend, Carl went out for a walk, jumped off a bridge, and killed himself. His body was found floating on the top of the water. I blamed myself, because I knew I had no right leaving for the weekend, since I was not stable. If only I'd stayed, Carl would have been alive. I carried that burden for years.

It is amazing to me that he felt alone, among other things, and that his loneliness led to hopelessness, which led to his suicide. It is disturbing to think that anyone that young would believe that their giants were so insurmountable, that they could not be conquered. There were some things that Carl obviously failed to tell me. In just one weekend by himself, Carl felt that the only answer to his problems was suicide. What was going through Carl's mind that was so troubling that he ended his life? What kind of silent anguish was Carl feeling that he could not tell me? We talked numerous times and while I felt we were close, obviously not close enough. This is an unfortunate reality of what happens when we don't talk about what is really going on with us. Men especially have this problem. We go in caves of privacy and sometimes never come out. Whatever his giants were, they were left far too long without enough empowering mental opposition. Carl was about eighteen years old.

Our teenagers are our future, and (yet a major part of our society would put them in jail for life, without the possibility of parole). I am not saying that a teen that kills should not be punished, but life in jail is not justice. Life in jail for a teen does not solve the problem or answer the question of why a young man would kill in the first place. Instead of throwing away the key when our young people do something stupid, we need to focus on rehabilitation. Children are being rejected and molested by people in authority who are supposed to love them. When they act out, we want to give up on them. We have to take more responsibility for the children in our society, because we live in it and we are their examples. So if the family is not reaching the child, then the village has to. The village is the extended family which consists of Pastors, mentors, teachers, community leaders and churches. I did not express a lot of my core feelings to my mother because she was a woman and I felt as if, a woman could not help a man with the issues of manhood. I did, however, express my emotions to my mentor. Most children are not going to express everything, to their parents because a lot of parents are not in their current world. They want someone they know who understands what they're going through and what they feel. That is why we must strike a common chord in a creative way. That's what entertainers do, and that is why they reach them so effectively.

It only takes one day, one moment, for things to change. That can either work for you or against you. So many people's giants have caused others, hurt, anger, and pain. By not killing your giants, they are not just affecting you, but others around you. Teenagers have giants. In August of this year, Boston Herald front page read, "Summer Of Wailing Mothers." The numerous murders on Boston streets committed by young people have caused a lifetime of pain and change for mothers. Some mothers have lost their children to violent deaths, while others have lost them to prison cells. What is unfortunate and unfair is that, it is not always the children's fault. Children are usually a product of their environment. If positive behavior was not modeled for them, then someone in their lives dropped the ball.

We live in a very reactive society. Traffic lights and stop signs are sometimes not put in place until an accident occurs or someone nearly dies. The church has been preaching sexual abstinence for years, but it was looked at as if it were a crazy idea. The argument was that, we are sexual beings, and we should be able to express ourselves sexually and explore sex with whomever we want because it is natural. Now that we have over forty million people with AIDS and other incurable, sexually transmitted diseases, we put ads on Television saying to our teens that it is cool to wait and be abstinent.

When I first saw those commercials, I laughed— not at the attempt but at the tardiness of the message. Sure, better late than never, but how many people have we lost and how many have been terribly affected before we started preaching the right thing? How many years did it the government to start putting out stronger and more explicit ads that say smoking kills you? We wait until it becomes one of the leading killers in America before we start to get aggressive. Another trend was obesity.

We cannot continue to preach a message that says, do whatever you want as long you feel good. A lot of movie producers and entertainers say it is only entertainment. Yet they know the power of subliminal messages and the power of catchy phrases, especially when put to music. They do not care about the images and messages they produce. Some people debate what is right and what is wrong based on opinion not principle. For every thing that we do, there are actions and consequences. There are penalties and rewards for our actions.

Here are some disturbing statistics and reasons for what happens when we do not kill our giants:

❏ The number of black men in jail have grown fivefold in the past twenty years. There are more black men in jail then in college and universities. [5]

❏ The United States has the highest prison population in the world.[6]

❏ In America, a woman is raped every 2 minutes.[7]

❏ Victims of marital or date rape are 11 times more likely to be clinically depressed, 6 more times more likely to experience social phobia than non victims. Psychological problems are still evident in cases as long 15 years after the assault. [8]

❏ 40 million people have been diagnosed with AIDS.[9]

❏ 45 percent of black men have never been married.[10]

❏ 42 percent of black women have never been married.[11]

With each statistic you could play the game of "Name That Giant." Why is it that almost 50 percent of black men have never been married? Is it fear of commitment? If we only make up 12 percent of the population, then why are we filling our prisons? What is wrong with men in general? Why are we so prone to violence? Is there a cry for help but no one is listening? The Bible says that there is a way that seems right to man but in the end, it leads to destruction. I continue to find it interesting that the Bible speaks to any situation and can be used for effective change if people allow it. The cost for not killing giants is way too high. Your destiny is awaiting you. I urge you to change the world by changing yourself.

Jesus died on the cross of Calvary a long time ago for you and me so that we might have total freedom at every level of life. You cannot win a spiritual battle by using human intellect. If you would say this simple prayer, the almighty God will save you right where you are: "Lord Jesus, I confess that I am a sinner in need of Your help. I turn from my ways to follow You for the rest of my life. Change me, save me, wash me. I believe with my heart and confess with my mouth that You are God and You raised Jesus Christ from the dead for my sins. So right now, by faith, I confess with my mouth that from this day forth Jesus is my Lord. Thank You, Jesus, for saving me."

According to Romans 10:9-10, if you confess that prayer my friend, you are saved. You now need to tell someone supportive about the most important and wonderful decision you have made. It is the first day of the rest of your life. Happy birthday!

In Closing

It is my simple hope and prayer that this book has been and will be a blessing to you. My desire is that you would really know God in a personal way and know that He desires to do a great work in you. I reference Scripture because they hold powerful truths that can be applied to all situations of life. I credit Him because it was never my intention to write a book. I am overwhelmed that He would give someone like me a book on such a subject to share with the nation. God is awesome, and He shows no favoritism. Please don't put God in a box like many do. Don't try to intellectualize and compartmentalize God; that will be your biggest mistake. Rather, approach Him with humility and with childlike faith, and He will do immeasurably more than you can ask or think in your life. *Your dreams are accessible and can come true if you believe.* Yes, there will always be giants trying to hinder you from your Promised Land, but **if your dreams are worth pursuing, then your giants are worth killing**. Pursue your Promised Land! May God richly bless you. Live your dreams!

About the Author

David Carruthers was born in Nottingham England. He is a gifted singer and songwriter who has performed extensively in the Boston area and has been featured at the House of Blues. David has been writing songs and poetry since the age of thirteen. He has written more than one hundred songs, and several have been published. The song, "Tell of his goodness" written for Regina Wingate was a number one hit in Bermuda. A number of his poems have been recognized by the International Poets Society. He has also opened for gospel greats such as Fred Hammond, Hezekiah Walker and Witness. He is a passionate motivational speaker and an anointed worship leader, who is often used in the prophetic. He is currently working on his first CD entitled "Journey", due next year. David is married with four children and currently lives in the Boston area, and Kill Your Giants is his first book. For speaking engagements and to find out more about David Carruthers, please call Alphonse Knight@ 617-282-8881 or visit his website at www. ciaministries.net.

Endnotes

Chapter 5

[1] Rich, F. (2001). *How Big is Porn?* [Electronic version]. *Forbes.com.* Retrieved from Web site: www.forbes.com/2001/05/25/0524porn.html.

[2] *American Rape Statistics.* (n.d.). Retrieved August 8, 2006, from Web site: http://www.paralumun.com/issuesrapestats.htm

Chapter 6

[3] Pryor, MD., D., *Suicide: Life's Curtain of Darkness*, Retrieved on September 6, 2006 from Black Womens Health, Web site: http://www.blackwomenshealth.com/suicide.htm

Chapter 8

[4] Brualdi, A. C. (1996). Muliple Intelligences: Gardner's theory. Washington, D": ERIC Clearinghouse on Assessment and Evaluation. [ED410226] Retrieved from Web site: http://chiron.valdosta.edu/whuitt/files/gardner.html.

Chapter 13

[5] Meritt, J. (2002, August 28). *Dramatic Rise in Number of Black Men in Prison. TalkLeft.* Retrieved from Web site: http://www.talkleft.com/new archives/00316.html.

[6] Walmsley, R. (2005). *World Prison Population List.* Retrieved September 2, 2006, from King's College London, International Centre for Prison Studies Web site: http://www.csa.nsw.gov.au/downloads/world-prison-population_list_2005.pdf

[7] *American Rape Statistics.* (n.d.). Retrieved August 8, 2006, from Web site: http://www.paralumun.com/issuesrapestats.htm

[8] Web site: http://www.paralumun.com/issuesrapestats.htm

[9] Quinn,T. C., Overbaugh, J. (2005). *HIV/AIDS in Women: An Expanding Epidemic. Science, [Electronic], 308(5728),* 1582-1583. Abstract Retrieved from Web site: http:www.sciencemag.org/cgi/content/abstract/308/5728/1582.

[10] *The shocking state of Black marriage: experts say many will never get married.* (n.d.). Retrieved September 4, 2006, from *Find Articles,* Web site http://www.findarticles.com/p/articles/mi m1077/is 1 59/ai 110361377.

[11] Find Articles, Web site: http://www.findarticles.com/p/articles/mi m1077/is 1 59/ai 110361377.